The Body of Christ

The Body of Christ

Sebastian Moore

with Kate Wilson

DARTON · LONGMAN + TODD

First published in 2011 by
Darton, Longman and Todd Ltd
1 Spencer Court
140–142 Wandsworth High Street
London SW18 4JJ

ISBN: 978-0-232-52857-2

A catalogue record for this book is available from the British Library.

Phototypeset by Kerrypress Ltd, Luton, Bedfordshire

Printed and bound in Great Britain by Page Bros, Norwich, Norfolk

Contents

Editor's Preface

Sebastian Moore OSB is into his tenth decade, living out a vocation that's a millennium and a half old, yet still profoundly challenging. Thirty years after *The Fire and the Rose Are One*, Sebastian's work reached a whole new generation in *The Contagion of Jesus*. This book is based on pieces written since then, some published on a blog, but mostly circulated by email to friends or handed out after chapel in Sebastian's Benedictine community at Downside.

The text is woven around the Passion, from the fear and betrayal of Maundy Thursday to the explosion of joy on resurrection morning. Sebastian tells the story again in a way that is highly aware of power and bodies, with exciting results.

Christ's body is offered in love for our divinely imaged bodies. Yet we live in a world and with a Church that doesn't always know how best to reflect this. Whether responding to individual despair and isolation, to the abuse crisis, institutional homophobia or clerical celibacy, to the latest papal visit or encyclical, Sebastian says things that need to be said, and heard.

This book draws on a stellar range of philosophers and theologians, from Aquinas and Eckhart to Girard and Alison. Each chapter is guided by a few (italicised) words from the editor, seeking to give the reader a way into these ideas. These are the product of a long conversation process, where each conversation partner saw different things in the text. The reader will surely find yet more food for conversation.

It has been a privilege to share the excitement of fresh ideas, to respond to the latest news from the global church, to watch thoughts take shape as each successive verse or sermon developed from the one before, as this book grew over the last two years. As we chose the pieces, citations from Sebastian's latest interest became my email signature for a while. They always resonated, in the most surprising places, with people who were so busy they had time to read nothing longer than a Facebook status update.

I hope that this book will do the same, and that you find as much to discover, to comfort and confront, as I did.

In this format as in so much, I am indebted to Stephen McCarthy who handed this project over to me. I would like to thank him for his help throughout. Thank you also to Brendan Walsh at DLT for his unfailing enthusiasm and support, to Jennifer Wild for her patience in shaping the final text. Thank you most of all to the community of inspiring and supportive women at the Margaret Beaufort Institute of Theology in Cambridge, for believing that 'nothing is impossible for God'.

Dr Kate Wilson
Cambridge
January 2011

Introducing a New Book:
The Shudder of Blissful Truth

What do we want? Why do we want? Ever since I began to think and to write and to try to pray, desire has been my question. Well obviously we want to be happy, yes blissful. But do we, really? Do you? Do I? Something in me says No to this desire, especially if theology comes along and says that this bliss we're after is limitless. That something may be called antibliss, and it is stronger in some than in others. It is 'the long sad tale of our humanity', and it says 'be sad, sad is safe'. Very recently an article in the *Guardian* suggested that people today *want* bad news.

So if our limitless desire is to become real in us, reality itself has massively to overcome this deep-seated No in us. We have to be 'shuddered' into this reality of ourselves and our world. The word is not in the OED, but we know it well. And every single instance in the Bible of God or great angel appearing, this presence introduces itself with the words 'Fear not!' The ultimate reality knows it's too much for us. In the Tolle moment, which for ten years has been crucial for me, full awareness was accompanied with 'intense fear' that stopped instantly when he obeyed the inner injunction to 'resist nothing'. Then he let himself fall into the void, and sleep, whence he awoke into a world of vision.

If the infinite bliss that I desire to be in ever *meets* the desire in me, this meeting has to be an overwhelming one. I believe that I have been overwhelmed, sporadically, and in this book I am inviting you to believe that you can be and perhaps have been.

The reality we call the Good News is that God is infinite bliss and is trying to win us over to himself. The obstacle is all that we mean by the cross. And the Good News in sum is that the cross has God's own Son on it, so formidable is our belief in the *bad* news.

Desire and its hazards provide, I think, the human context in which the resurrection of our victim from the dead best appears as the gateway to ultimate bliss, and recovers its meaning from two millennia of lazy repetition and ecclesial triumphalism.

Sebastian Moore
Downside Abbey
March 2011

1

Thursday Evening – Broken Bread, Broken Bodies

Christ creates a moment of belonging, connecting us in a shared meal to which we can always reconnect, offering his body to be broken and bring us into communion.
(Fitzpatrick's 'In Breaking of Bread'[1])

Real food, a real meal for real bodies – the Eucharist presents us with a real challenge.

As Irenaeus said, 'the glory of God is a human being fully alive', and we are never more alive than when we are fully present in our own bodies, aware of how we belong to each other.

Christ offers his own body for us, becoming more fully human than we could dare to risk, perhaps too human for us to bear. At the Last Supper, the first Eucharist, Jesus prepares his friends for the breaking of his body on the cross by breaking it for them first.

The church constantly needs to recall this basic human act of breaking bread. Christ shares food with his friends, and the Eucharist should be remembered in this way, as a shared meal, not a distant liturgical ritual. As Jesus himself tells us, his flesh is real food, and this reality can be hard to face. Yet it is a liberating truth; the reality of Christ's body gives dignity to our own bodies, making us more fully human.

For this we can give thanks, stopping to breathe and remember within the human body that God gave us and shared with us.

1.1 Belonging: An Exercise in Being Human

Finding your place in God means starting within yourself, entering into an empty space where you can see yourself and others as they really are, in their own shape and form. Creating space for each one to be as they are creates space for belonging together. Practising this ourselves reveals the God who is already there.

Have I a purpose in this world? Before considering this question, let me go into myself, sink down into the void of creativity and then wonder at this void, let it be beautiful to sink in and be born of into the form I have. See other people, as we all do, in *their* forms. Then apply to them your own sense of detachment from form. Mentally see others free of their forms and enjoy with them the coming-to-be out of the void.

Then ask, is all this exercise quite pointless? If it seems so, do it again!

If it is not pointless, what is the point of it? At least it is an exercise in being human.

Now notice that in this exercise in being human, the other humans are involved. The way down is a way shared, the way down into shared depths.

Is this whole exercise futile? I don't think it is possible to do the exercise and still find it pointless. The exercise comes into play when I ask, do I have a reason for being in this world? For being *with* this world, because when you think of yourself at any depth you are thinking of yourself-in-the world. The image of 'world' becomes clear to me. It is more and it is ours. The more you keep on this wavelength, the more indissolubly bound together we are.

Now ask again, do I have a reason to be in this world? The answer yes *includes* the world and the people in it, the people of it.

If it appears to me that I with us have a reason to be in this world, is there a *step* I need to take if I find that I and we have a purpose? This step will consist in *affirming* that I and we, I among us, have a purpose.

This step of affirming me in us is a step about belonging. Now what it means to belong to the church is not like joining an association or club. The church is not a club. It is humanity self-affirming as purposive in the world.

And what of this acknowledged sharing in the purpose to be? This whole exercise, the more it is pursued, is *implying* that the meaning of it is real, is. If you like, it is the being in which we all are. It is the will that we be.

The interesting thing about this exercise is that God emerges as its meaning, as our meaning. In *this* context, the question 'is there a God?' is missing the point, for it is implicitly defining, understanding, 'God' *not* as 'the meaning of it all' but as a being out there who might or might not

exist. What I am suggesting is the exercise in self and other, appropria-
tion for which the question 'is there a God?' *does not arise*. The meaning
that God is is already there – or not there if the exercise is thought to be
pointless.

1:2 A Shared Meal: A Love-Feast

*Christ shows us how to be more human by sharing food with us on Thursday
evening. This is not a liturgical performance to be celebrated at a distance,
restoring the ritual that Christ sought to overcome. It is a real meal to be shared
by all the people, a joyful 'love-feast' of human freedom and belonging.*

'O Sacrum Convivium'[2]

Aquinas' most acclaimed description of the Eucharist is in the Anthem
'*O Sacrum Convivium!*' Now a *convivium* is a love-feast, and that is what
the sacrament of the Passion is. The more we allow the sacred *convivium*
to resonate through the whole history of humanity in the one universal
anthropological event, the shared meal, the more we see how wrong is
this denial, to the sacrament of the sacrifice, of the character of a meal.

The way the word sacrifice behaves in the wretched account of a
theology that became conventional is what has led a perceptive theologian to describe it as the most treacherous word in the Christian vocabulary.[3] The divinity of the victim, far from conferring sacrificial status on
Calvary, dissolves it.[4] This revisionary transformation of the word sacrifice makes the *true* sacrifice our food *before* Jesus identifies the bread as
his body. It creates for us a newly symbolised reality, 'the bread of life'.
'The bread of life' – who ever heard of that? – nourishes something new
in us, the true self evoked by the vindicated, non-vindictive and forgiving victim impressing on the soul of the disciple the risen condition of
having died into life beyond life. Jesus feeds the soul not metaphorically
but by bestowing the food that 'the eternal in man' – to quote Scheler[5] –
needs. This rooting of the Eucharistic meal in the emancipation from
sacrificial religion is conveyed by the liturgy properly performed and
understood, that shows its nourishing character from the very start of
the ritual.

The huge labour called the liturgical movement, a real awakening of
the church before, and to culminate in, the Council, was to expose and
dispose of this loose end, and offer people, for the first time for most of
our history, the sacramental entry into the sacrifice of Jesus. And the key

idea round which this recovery ordered itself was that Jesus, on the night before he suffered, took the bread, broke it and shared it as 'my body for you', and the cup likewise. In other words, he used the oldest and only universal symbol of the community that God sees us as, a shared meal.

That this idée-mère has opened the Mass to trivialisation I do not doubt. But, as a remedy, to abandon it as what the Mass is, and implicitly to readmit the para-sacramental sacrificial meaning, the Mass as the drama of Calvary re-enacted, is surely a desperate move.

Reform of the reform?

Bread broken and shared, wine blessed and shared, is a meal. Period. But we learn from Jungmann, who is the chief authority, that very soon the emphasis shifted from the rite as meal to the rite as defined by the solemn prayer of thanksgiving, and it is on this early shift that the present Pope's strong disagreement with a meal-centred theology is based.

But surely it is clear that the finding, in the Eucharistic Prayer, of what Ratzinger brilliantly calls a transformation of existence – even of death – into thanksgiving, is simply the discovery of what in this meal is wholly special and indeed unique. It is not a de-emphasising of the fact that it *is* a meal. This de-emphasising is a further stage, and it has been reached when the Eucharistic Prayer is being described as a quasi-holy place and named as the Holy of Holies, to be entered by the priest alone, with the people as outsiders or spectators. This development does not follow from, is not pre-contained in, the experienced transformativeness of the Eucharistic Prayer. On the contrary, it would naturally resonate in the hearts of the people in whose name the priest is giving thanks. For its failure to do this, we have to look to another source, and the most likely one is the amazing phenomenon whereby the faith that created martyrs became the state religion. For with this, to be a Christian is no longer necessarily to be a disciple, but to be a decent citizen.

In an important article, 'Benedict XVI and the Eucharist',[6] Eamon Duffy writes:

> It seemed therefore that the Eucharist's basic structure was unequivocally that of a meal, and this was the position adopted by Guardini and most other theorists of liturgical reform from the 1930s onwards. Immediately however, the dogmatic theologians detected a problem. Was not this pre-

cisely the position Luther had adopted in renaming the Mass the Lord's Supper, and hence, was not this the view condemned at Trent? Did not an account of the Mass as in essence a meal reduce or obliterate its sacrificial character?

Ratzinger's answer is unequivocally yes. He argues that

> the Eucharistic thesis [that it is thanksgiving and not meal that defines the Mass] is able to put the dogmatic and liturgical levels in touch with each other. For the Eucharistic thanksgiving is the form [this, and not the meal, he means] in which Jesus at his Last Supper attached sacrificial meaning to his death, and identified the elements of bread and wine with his flesh and blood given for the forgiveness of sins ... the Eucharistic words of Jesus are the transformation of existence – even of death – into thanksgiving.[7]

This is beautiful. Ratzinger is saying that that which identifies the bread and wine with Jesus' body and blood – which of course is the crucial step – and makes a feeling-sense of this identification, makes doxological sense if you like, is the prayer that is celebrating the victory over death, a paean of life beyond life as we know it. This is Ratzinger, and I'm with it all the way. But why does this transformation of existence, even of death, into thanksgiving, into Eucharist, in a uniquely appropriate doxology, which gives us at last, yes, the sacrifice *convincingly* in bread and wine, have to reduce to secondary status the fact that what we have here is food and drink shared, the new *convivium*, indeed the Supper of the Lamb, the sacred meal that is the cult of Christians? It doesn't follow, surely.

And so much is at stake here. The language in which, indeed, liturgy and doctrine are in touch with each other so that we have take-off, does take off – and leave the wondering people behind! It is indeed an endlessly fascinating problem – it has exercised me most of my thinking life – as to how we get, in a way of feeling, from the bread and wine to the awesome reality of Calvary made luminous by Easter, and the alchemy that Ratzinger finds in the Thanksgiving Prayer really pulls this off, I think. It gets me thinking-together these chosen foodstuffs of his ritual and a new earth, but saying *how* this makes sense, how this conjoins bread-and-wine and a new world born on the cross, does not swallow up the bread and wine as food and drink, as meal, about which all these wonderful things are being said, the doxologically sacred meal.

Is there a confusion between the natural coming-to-the-fore of the rite in the solemn Thanksgiving with the subsequent *interpretation* of this development as making of the Great Prayer a quasi-Holy-of-Holies to be entered by the priest alone, the people outside?

Once this confusion is overcome, it makes perfect sense to see the Mass as a ritual meal in which the participants, with understanding faith, hear the celebrant utter the Great Prayer that 'transforms existence – even of death – into thanksgiving'. The fact that this is not often a description of what happens with the reformed rite leads me to a radical question: is Jesus too human for us? Choosing as the ritual of his passage our oldest and the only universal symbol, the meal shared, he exposes that most human thing to our banality.

And it is just here that there occurs to me what Alexander Schmemann, the great Orthodox theologian, names as the 'Eucharistic Crisis, eastern and western': 'the loss of the Assembly'. The Assembly is lost in the beautiful words that are lost on the Assembly.

Nearly seventy years ago, Gregory Dix, in *The Shape of the Liturgy*,[8] pointed out that with the Christianising of the Empire, being a Christian changed from being a disciple, with one's life at risk, to being a respectable citizen. One effect of this, he said, would surely have been that full participation in the rite fell to the celebrant, the professional as it were. As the bishops changed from martyrs to people with competence and power, so the people changed from communicants to 'the people at Mass', their 'Easter Duties' being to communicate once a year. I remember as a pious child being surprised at this Commandment of the Church. Only once a year? Another surprise, that came much later as I was 'doing my theology', was that one of the demands voiced by the Pilgrimage of Grace under Henry VIII was a return to the old Mass at which only the priest communicated, this latter detail being specified.

Now let us take a big leap, to the innovative advocacy of frequent communion by Pius X, the full significance of which has only just dawned on me. It is not only saying 'the more the better', a good prescription for spiritual health. It also means the normality of the congregation communicating at the Mass, which makes the Mass more evidently a ritual meal, though one of unique moment.

And now another connection begins to appear, between 'the Mass not evidently a ritual meal' and 'the Mass clericalised'. If the old rite does mark the beginning of the clericalising of the liturgy, then to advocate its restoration is to advocate a re-clericalising; and after all, in the old rite the celebrant does play all the roles.

This leads me to invoke, in conclusion, a ground-breaking book on the Mass that appeared in 1993, *In Breaking of Bread* by P. F. Fitzpatrick, a priest I came to know well. This was, far and away, the best book on the Mass that I had ever read – and I read the lot in those days! – and this goes for everyone to whom I have recommended it. The book is ground-breaking in that it discloses the role of ritual in our lives at a depth that we are not normally conscious of. The Mass is, most radically, a ritual. It is His ritual. A ritual what? A ritual meal. Let the author speak for himself:

> 'Do this in memory of me': Luke's Gospel agrees with Paul's account in First Corinthians in having Jesus give that command to those who were eating with him at the Last Supper. The early testimony of Justin Martyr (*c.*180 AD), which also records it, shows that the story was taken then by Christians as including a command to carry out a ritual eating and drinking. What Aquinas has to say about Christ's choice of the occasion is worth setting down at the start of this section [on the way of ritual]:
>
>> The last things to be said, especially by friends who are about to leave us, are those that are best remembered. At such a time, our love for our friends is greatest; and what we love most is what sinks deepest into our hearts.[9]

This leads me to my conclusion. I am with the Pope in seeing that the Great Prayer 'transforms existence – even death into thanksgiving', and I find this extraordinarily beautiful. I am not with him in saying that this makes the Prayer, and not the sharing, say what the Mass is.

Finally, the implication that, in tying his apotheosis to a shared meal, Jesus is too human for us, has enormous ramifications. It sends us back, for his ritual, to his Jewish origins, whether of temple or table, and on back to our emergence as a species, mimetically desirous and so prone to sharing of food, not just getting it. And it sends us on to the Reformation as articulating the need to *restore* the shared meal as the Lord's Supper. I recall the author of *Fearful Symmetry*[10] saying that there are only three symbols that are universal, beyond our archetypes: the notion of sexual union as holy, of the shared meal as uniting us with divinity, and the image of life as a journey. Reading the way in which Catholic theologians write about Protestant ones where liturgy is concerned, one cannot but be struck by an unconsciously militant provincialism: we have a sacrifice, they don't – this suggests the playground rather than the theological discussion. The whole idea of 'looking for a sacrifice' in Protestant worship and probably not finding it is pitiable. Even Duffy, a most sophisticated historian, can note, as a sufficient objection to the meal-paradigm, that that's what Luther said, so it won't do – this is playground talk. In this tragic, and according to Martin Rees, final age of humanity,[11] we have to shrug off such puerilities, and, in the breaking of the bread, given us by our trans-human model, we have the holding-ground for this not to amount to absurdity and anarchy. This is a case for the anthropologist or the sociologist, rather than the theologian: where religion is concerned, we're still children.

But now, even here, we have to grow up.

1.3 Real Food: Becoming Christ's Body

Christ says, 'this is my body, this is my blood' – this is real food to sustain us and transform us into Christ's body. On Thursday evening Christ offers his body to us, before it is offered on the cross on Friday afternoon, making the sacrifice fruitful. To understand what this sacrifice really means, we need to put this real eating and drinking back at the centre of our celebration of the Eucharist.

The crucifixion was a human sacrifice offered by the powers of this world religious and secular, whose rule has death as its instrument – its baton as one Jewish writer calls it – under the aegis of Caiaphas the High Priest. This sacrifice of our humanity to the powers that be is, by its victim, stood on its head, in such wise that the victim, in defiance of the prime requirement for sacrifice of the non-personhood, the thingness of the victim, is protagonist and priest. As priest, he has his ritual, with bread and wine, which he declares to be his body and his blood for us to share in. His commentary on this action is given in the Eucharistic sermon in John chapter 6, in which he says 'unless you eat the flesh of the Son of Man and drink his blood, you do not have [his] life in you', and goes on to accentuate the meal-character of what he is advancing by insisting 'my flesh is food indeed, my blood is drink indeed.' If that statement is not Eucharistic realism, nothing is!

In saying what he says at the supper, he shows us his way of drawing us into himself as priestly victim, so that we become what we eat and drink, not only turning it into ourselves as we do with all food and drink but turning us into it, as Augustine intuited when he heard, 'I am the food of grown people.'[12]

A great deal is involved here and comes together, and the hard focus is the victim-protagonist-priest, a ritual with bread and wine being his way, unique in the history of religion everywhere, of drawing what we can manage of selfless love into his huge priestly victimhood. *To* our oldest and our only universal ritual – we don't all marry but we all eat and drink together – he gives a significance without parallel in religion, the scandal of the sermon in John 6. To this universal ritual of food and drink shared, he gives unique significance in identifying these with his own flesh and blood crucified.

And how does Jesus show himself as victim who breaks the rule of the victim, whose essence is passivity, non-personhood, nobody-ness, magnificently in being on the contrary the protagonist and priest of *his* sacrifice, saying in John, 'you do not take my life, I lay it down of myself.' And when, over the bread, he says '*my* body', and, over the cup, '*my* blood', we have to get deeper and deeper into this vision of the speaking and sharing victim-protagonist. We have to let Jesus dismantle all our cultic sacrificial categories in giving us the food of grown men and women that transforms us into him our true self.

This is one of those extraordinary Jesus-realities that I keep discovering anew.

In conclusion, might there be a hitherto undiscovered salvific name for what Calvary does with our standard method of securing peace of a sort by the sacrifice of a scapegoat? A salvific name, indeed, such that – to be even more ambitious – the victim in whom this transcending of our scapegoating is achieved would want to be participated in with the oldest and only universal ritual we have, the ritual meal. And just as his sacrifice stands our sacrificing on its head and transforms it into a revelatory new humanity, our participation in it would stand the action of food and drink on its head so that *this* food transforms us into itself. The Eucharist is his special ritual, and the elucidation of it is his: 'you are to eat my flesh and drink my blood and so have life in me. I who re-form all religion am religiously sacrificed and, against religion's claim on God, vindicated as are vindicated religion's victims into a love that dissolves vindictiveness and the righteousness it represents.' One gets a glimpse of what might be meant by Paul's saying in Romans that the righteousness of God is revealed on the cross.

What is central is the participation that this invites, the boundless love of a human flourishing out of anguish. When the risen one on the road to Emmaus says, 'Did not the Christ have to suffer all this?' he is pointing to something much more than Plato is pointing to in this astonishingly circumstantial account: 'The just man, then, as we have pictured him, will be scourged, tortured, and imprisoned, his eyes will be put out, and after enduring every humiliation, he will be crucified.'[13] The stranger on the Emmaus Road is inviting us to the *Sacrum Convivium*.

Always I come back to the point, that the true statement of Eucharistic realism is our Lord's: 'eat my flesh and drink my blood, because my flesh is real food and my blood is real drink.' How extraordinary it is that to achieve *our* realism we have to leave out eating and drinking, or at least leave it merely implied.

On John's Gospel chapter six

You said, 'my flesh is food, my blood your drink,'
They found this a hard saying, what of us
Who are bewildered as to how to think
But know you as our victim glorious?

And you went on, 'what will you think when I
Return to being by my Father's side,'
But in the meantime you will crucify
Me as the victim of our human pride.

And that's how you returned to where you were
And where were we who left you and betrayed?
Nowhere until we saw you, heart to stir
And for the first time we were not afraid,

So with fear gone we know your Eucharist
As meaning that we otherwise have missed.

1.4 Body for our Bodies

Christ's human body, which was broken for us, gives dignity to our human bodies and makes them whole. We are connected to each other as members of the one Body of Christ. This reminds us of our need to go within, to recognise our own desires so that we can recognise and truly encounter each other, so that love can happen.

How is the Body of Christ not an abstraction? I must be able to feel it. What did Bishop Robinson mean when he said that Paul's meaning for the Body of Christ is not corporate but corporal? He was unable to say, but he heard Paul in this sense.

Approaching this question from my end, the best discovery I have made is that there is a way, in a conflictual situation, so to empathise with myself in the conflict as to feel us 'both in the same boat' of this confusion. Now this is a sense of my body extending somehow into another's body.

Most important is the change that comes about when I destabilise 'my desires', acknowledging with J. M. Oughourlian that they are not mine, they well up in me as the desires of others past and present.[14] As I get into the habit of questioning and perhaps welcoming desire, of thinking of desire as a movement I can flow with instead of claiming it as my own, I am becoming open to a new attitude to a work of art, which ceases to be an object that I judge; rather *it* addresses *me* and, as Rilke says, under this address 'I must change my life,' my cosy life that the painting is now looking at. As you go into the Louvre you see a notice, 'You do not judge the paintings: they judge you.' I notice, in looking at a new picture, a kind of impatience, even resentment at the attention it is calling for. Let that go, let the painting be!

All this suggests a rich ebullient life that I am *in*. I am now extending the range of my tenderness inclusive of the tenderness of another with whom I am having difficulties. This experience, I now see, is not an isolated or privileged insight, but rather my acquaintance with the Body as alive in me (one of its members, Paul will make bold to say).

Now this suggests a new way of thinking about the familiar Pauline statement that when one member suffers the others suffer with it. In this way, no reasoning has to take place between the report of a friend's loss and pain and my prayer for him. In the body as I now learn to inhabit it, I can feel his loss and some of his pain. I am 'in the body' as I am 'in touch', 'in one system of communication'.

This was brought home to me recently when a friend told me of a separation from his wife. It took the form of my *recognising* that I was glad it wasn't me, this brutally reinforced by a dream in which he was giving me a nice surprise! – with such candour does the unconscious expose us to ourselves. I'm sure the disciple of Jesus was glad it wasn't him as Jesus was led away. But this confessing of my ego's response aided the prevailing of a deeper fellow-feeling that I am describing. 'Rejoice with those who rejoice, weep with those who weep' is not a saying at the level of a sympathy card. It's a description of life in the Body, the life of those who are painfully coming alive in a world so full of death and fear and death-dealing.

What is meant by 'going with the flow' is letting desire in me not be something conjured up when I see something I want, a well-advertised product, but a movement that wells up inside me. This predisposes me, in a gallery, to let the paintings speak as opposed to looking at them impatiently, resenting their demand. What this change amounts to is unseating the censor of the impatient ego, giving space to artists' love trying to happen. Love is people happily together, as opposed to looking impatiently at each other. I find I am trying to convey a new feel in me.

In the Body

The body hugs itself, the feel of me
As I am loved into to be by you
With all my brothers, sisters, amity
Where being is equated with the true.

The self acquisitive is not alone:
Inquisitive I know another way
Of longing for you utterly unknown
That eases me as I find I can pray.

The body hugs itself: how do I know
To say this and immediately to feel
Love's tenderness upon the breath as so
Where each pretence reveals itself as peel.

I know love woke in me, for I succumbed
Without all doubt, I previously numbed.

1.5 Thanksgiving

To return to the beginning of this chapter – Eucharist is a thanksgiving for love, which we can feel and participate in again, when we make enough space to allow ourselves to feel our emptiness, to make space for the dangerously too-human Christ to set us free.

I know a blank where I am tender, tending
It has a time that I look forward to,
In it a useless past finds its own mending
In thankfulness that is addressed to 'you'.

When I read of another who fell so
I knew him and he gave me words to say it,
My blank became the void where forms we know
Are born, and I am given words to pray it

That come out of a dangerous memory
Of those who met your Jesus, victim, risen.
The blank in me was you making us free
He leading all our kind out of its prison.

The thanks that come to me as I vacate
Are Eucharist, the word of those who wait.

Memory of Me

Now let the bread bare him and be the whole
To catch me up into his sacrifice
Which at the start of all silently stole
Up on our violence which has its price

And altered it, the altar of the cross
Revealed our holocaust as murderous
For the forgiveness of us at a loss
Which I come into now with all of us

As we partake of the remembered bread
And wine and come into our opened eyes
That see our victim risen from the dead
Our Eucharist, contemplative surprise

I had, letting these eyes fall on him risen
And knew myself no longer in this prison.

2

Thursday Night – The Void in the Garden

The Agony in the Garden: Christ faces his own void at
Gethsemani. We have to face this letting-go of ego to
create a unified space through which God can work.
(Eckhart Tolle's moment[1])

*To be strengthened by the Body of Christ is to be prepared to go out into the night
with him. On Thursday night he takes his friends with him to face the void in
the garden, where he is taken prisoner to set us free ...*

*We have bodies which are good, and are affirmed by sharing real food – but we
also have minds, which we do not always know how to direct to the good.
Confronting the blank fear where the mind despairs and becomes disconnected
from embodied reality allows us to move into the ultimate reality which is God.
Facing the void is not easy. John Chapman OSB noticed that attention to God is
inattention to everything else – Sebastian connects his confrère's assertion to
Eckhart Tolle's 'moment' of befriending the void, letting go of his ego or
'pain-body'.*

*This is what Christ does in the garden of Gethsemani; by entering the void,
letting go, he lets love happen. This opens up an infinite space for transformation.*

*Christ invites his disciples in the garden to stay awake; staying awake is
becoming aware of the divine strength within. Staying awake is also learning to
let go – even of Christ himself, as he prepares for his death which is to come.*

2.1 Losing Friends: An Exercise in Being Alone

*Trying to pray only starts working when you stop trying. This is much easier to
say than to do. In Gethsemani, Christ tried to pray as never before, moving a
little distance away even from his closest friends, trying to let go of everything,
all desires, except for God, who is love.*

Our Abbot Chapman had a definition that has proved momentous. An act of attention to God, he said, is an act of inattention to everything else. Now for the mind to be without thought is not difficult. Tolle offers the experiment of sitting still, and raising your hand the moment a thought comes to you. You may be surprised that this takes quite a few seconds. But of course Chapman's inattention has a more serious intention, to do with the fact that, as Aquinas says, we do not know what God is, only what God is not. It is that unknown God that this blank in thought intends. Buddhism speaks of the void as where all the forms of things are born, and I find this idea very attractive – this attraction is the desire for God, I think.

Now here is a big step. We've been thinking about thinking. What about wanting? Try to make a list of things you want, and it goes on and on – money, sex, friendship, power, fun, and so on. Now let me tell you about the best idea I've ever had. It came to me teaching undergraduate theology in the United States: Desire is love trying to happen. I still don't know where it came from. When Carol, our secretary in Campus Ministry at Marquette University, saw it as the title of one of my sheets for students, she said, 'That's the only thing of yours I understand!' She spoke with enthusiasm, for she had a healthy suspicion about men. Desire is love trying to happen. One of our guests here, a theological busybody, reported this formula of mine to Rome, and the Head Prefect of the CDF got in touch with the Abbot! So the formula is gathering dust on a hit-list somewhere.

Now all wanting wants happiness, and the essence of happiness is being in love, not only romantically but totally, with all of yourself. Here's another big step. It's about a huge illusion we all have: that my desires are mine, that they start with me. Here's me, and there's that latest laptop, and I want it, period. But the truth is that my fixing on that laptop is only the desire for happiness coming into focus as I contemplate this little gem of technology and want it, the whole thing arranged by a refined technique of advertising. Desires happen to us. They bubble up from deep down in us, from family, gender, race, you name it. So my desire is what is happening to me. What is *trying* to happen is what it's all about, what *I* am all about, me in love, giving myself completely.

Now try putting together, try connecting, the non-attention to everything, the blank, the felt-for unknown that God is, and me with all my desires as love trying to happen, self-gift trying to happen, and we stumble on the big equation: between love trying to happen and God the unknown. The kind of praying that Abbot Chapman teaches[2] is an exercise along these lines, a quiet emptying of the mind coupled with a letting in of desire. When I was working in Marquette University, in Campus Ministry, we had a prayer group that met every Monday, and on one occasion, in the discussion that followed the hour of silence, someone asked: is there any difference between this centring prayer we do and Transcendental Meditation, TM? One young faculty member said: 'I did TM regularly as a relaxation exercise, and then after a time I found in this a sense of longing, which is prayer, I think.' He was a regular practising Catholic.

So here are two ideas, the God-blank and love trying to happen as the drive behind your desires, and they want to come together. The God-blank and love trying to happen in the midst of all my issues and worries.

It may be helpful if I tell you how it happened for me, in by far the most important event of my life. I'd already been a monk for three years, and I was doing my stint at what was called mental prayer. This consisted in half an hour morning and evening trying to pray on my own. We were taught to 'get it going' by repeating a helpful tag from a psalm or the *Confessions* of St Augustine. And it was torture. It just didn't work, and I did myself some brain damage – *not* a good monastic experience! Then the thought came – be honest! And I said to God, 'This is useless, I'm fed up and bored with the whole thing!' Now I still can't find the words for what *then* happened. Somehow a weight was lifted off my mind and I heard myself saying, 'I'll give you anything you want, I'm yours!' And then it was as if layer upon layer of my pretences was peeled away, and with each layer I said 'Yes, that too!' and with many backslidings it's been that way ever since. To put it briefly, I told God he bored me and I don't think he liked that, because he's never bored me since.

Now look, I would never have had the impertinence to tell you how God broke in on what James Alison, my great theologian friend, calls 'my smelly desires', if it were not that I now have a theory to explain the experience, the theory I've just given you that puts together the Chapman God-blank and 'desire is love trying to happen'. The theory, if you like, deprivatises my experience and makes it available. It gives you, I hope, an experiment you can try.

Chapman is so wonderful. He said to someone I knew well, 'My friends call me a Buddhist!' He was a thoroughly orthodox Catholic, as was Meister Eckhart, the medieval Dominican who said all sorts of God-blanky things.

2.2 Agony in the Garden: Let Go to Let Love

To let love happen, you have to let go. This is what Christ did in the garden of Gethsemani, letting go of his own ego, 'preferring to be loved to being me'. This is the way which he invites us to take.

Let go of me who want, and let be loved
This frightened me to which I have to cling
Let the revision of Gethsemani
Be all, me emptying of everything.
Just connect being loved with being free
As Jesus in the garden, now as me

Says yes to freedom from the things I want
And think they make me, clothe my nakedness
That is my lovedness as your garden me
Is mine, the loved and terrified to be:
What is the garden me but victim willing
The huge revision of a violent world
Shedding the myth of dominance in me
Who let it happen and myself be loved.
This is the attitude that liturgises
Lets happen in me the transforming will.

The secret: to be loved is to be free,
To let, to liturgise, identical
As a man proud of all he is and does
Will let someone be fond of him regardless
And be surprised into a self that loves.

This alchemy done in the darkened garden
Can be for me the self transformed in love.
It is made there for us in resurrection
When he was seen by souls that he had stripped
By his arrest and the succeeding horror
The resurrection a position gained
For all humanity to liturgise,
Start in the name of him who is the all
And then of him who is plunged in the shit*
And then of Holy Spirit to enthral.

All needed is a taste for poverty
Preferring to be loved to being me.
This is the formula of flourishing
Discovered as the myth of dominance
Gives way in joy to being this loved thing
Was made to come into the garden dance.
It isn't complicated, agony
When it is prayed by him in the dark garden
The formula unchanged: rather be loved
Than gain, just as he said, the world entire.
If I could only feel you under me.

or: God in heaven, God in hell, and God in all.

How Jesus in the garden does in me
Undoing of the will to dominate
In favour of the love that makes us free
Of fear that holds us in its awful state:

Let go of wanting so that I am loved
Into my being: but how is this willed
. By me: I have to let my heart be moved
On feeling loved with all desire stilled.

This is the Jesus-briefing in the garden
Under the Angel of the Agony,
Here will the heart of history unharden
And those who find the place of it will see

As they saw when he came upon their dread
And vanished in the breaking of the bread.

2.3 Befriend the Void

The void embraced by Christ clarifies the difference between the false self, the ego, and the true self. This does not mean a separation of the mind from the body, but that Christ feels through the body and transforms it into something greater – Christ's risen body includes us all as his members.

A theology unaware of the difference between ego and true self is hopeless, I think, especially when it comes to the crisis of faith that our Saviour undergoes at Gethsemani. For without the distinction, Gethsemani is a collision of wills, God's and man's, whereas the distinction enables us to intuit in Jesus a surrender of ego that is, of all that we know as life in this sinful world, to the sheer nothing out of which the Father is to create the world anew.

With amazing psychological perception, the Letter to the Hebrews says, in this context of the Saviour's choice of the cross for the joy it contained, that the word of God penetrates to the point of intersection of the mind and the Spirit! And with similar daring, the adventurous translation of John Henson – approved by Rowan Williams – describes the point of the Agony as follows:

> Jesus said, 'Loving God, please don't let me have to go through with this. But if it's what you want me to do, I'm ready.' As Jesus said this, he experienced a great upsurge of strength, and he knew God had not left him on his own. But the pain of grief and anxiety *was so intense as he opened his heart*, the sweat fell from him in great big drops.[3]

The body protests, by sweating blood, at a surrender demanded of it that outrages good sense and makes of it the body to be done to death, raised from the dead to have us all its members. 'As in one body there are the many members, so it is *with Christ*.' Not 'so it is with the body to which I am comparing the church' (2 Corinthians 13:4).

2.4 Pain-Body: Feeling Bad about Feeling Good

In the night at Gethsemani, Christ faces his own fear of death in order to overcome it. On the brink of suicide, Eckhart Tolle too befriended the void; by consenting to 'resist nothing', he could see his true self beyond his self-pitying ego. This false self, or pain-body, is quite simply 'feeling bad about feeling good'. Sebastian puts this in a Christian context; for him, the pain-body is the original sin from which Christ liberates.

It seems that there are two journeys that we need to take, from where I and you are, to where the church is with her liturgy, its high point of

Easter, and the journey the church has to take from its liturgical formulas to the reality of Jesus, our life now and for ever.

Now there is an experience given to our time, something that happened to Eckhart Tolle, that telescopes these two journeys into one.

Tolle awoke in the small hours, inundated with self-hatred, the accumulation of a life in search and beset with self-loathing. He decided to do away with himself, saying, 'I cannot any longer live with myself.' Then the thought came, 'This is an odd thing to say. Are there two of me, I and the self that "I" cannot live with?' Then came the thought, 'Maybe only one of them is real', and with this he was filled with terror and lay there shaking from head to foot, totally conscious with nothing to think about, all the old landmarks gone. It felt like he was being sucked inward, into a void, 'in a vortex of energy'. Then came the words 'Resist nothing!' He obeyed and surrendered – to be inundated with total peace for the first time in his life, a peace he has lived in ever since, adjusting himself to it as he did his job – he was a research chemist at Cambridge. With his surrender, he fell asleep, and was awakened a few hours later by the song of a bird and was overcome with its beauty and with the beauty of all his surroundings. Especially he felt the miracle of light.

Now Chapman says that an act of attention to God is an act of inattention to everything else. This definition plays a trick with the mind. It is a formula that teases the reason and trips up the mind so that, with luck, you stumble into the nothing that the formula implies, the opposite of 'everything', and this immediately seems right. Chapman helps when you read casually about 'nothing in particular, which is God of course', which nearly got him put in the Index of Prohibited Books.

Now there is clearly a similarity between the 'nothing' into which Tolle was sucked as he was violently disidentified with what he had always taken to be his life, and the 'nothing' you drop into when the Chapman formula takes and something in you sees the point. Untold numbers of people, religious and lay, have stumbled into contemplative prayer, as I did one evening, through this quasi-koan. And I am sure that many of Tolle's readers have identified his drastic demotion of the ego as the power in charge of awareness.

Now don't these two de-egoisings marry up nicely? They most certainly did for me, but of course I've practised the Chapman way for most of my monastic life. And Chapman has a considerable lay readership clerical and lay. Surely the connection is waiting to be made.

And once it is made, a wonderful result follows. The drop into the void matches with looking inward to Jesus dead and risen. When I was bowled over by Tolle about six years ago, I found that as, walking around our grounds, I envisaged Jesus dead and risen, I could pull the plug out of the inflatable toy of ego – Tolle's image. The connection came to me so easily, and I'm still amazed at this.

Now what was being required of him – and of us if we are to survive – is to live as one not two. For us disciples of Jesus, the true self discovered by Tolle has a name, *the* name: The Nazarene, *crucified* – of course! – by our violent world and raised from the dead to spread the happiness of God.

Now after a few years adjusting to life with this new consciousness, someone said to Tolle, 'I want what you have, can you give it me?' His reply is the answer to the question of the journey inward – and outward – with which I started this note: 'You have it already, only you can't feel it because your mind is making too much noise.'

Our journey into Easter is the journey beyond our world full of mental noise into a silence that, if you let faith in such as you have never had it before, is the silence of contemplative prayer.

Now Tolle made an astonishing discovery *about our mental noise*, at least about a great deal of it. It consists in talking to myself, the stories I tell myself about everything that goes on, about the people I live with and what happens. With a stroke of genius, he thought of these stories as me *feeding myself*. What exactly are they feeding? Well, is there something in me that wants to hear this kind of story? Self-pity is the word surely. But is there something in me that is *corroborated* by 'dismal stories' as Bunyan calls them? Well, it is something that *wants to hear them*. Is there perhaps in all of us something that I described years ago, on American radio: feeling bad about feeling good. Tolle calls this the pain-body, which he defines as an inherited addiction to unhappiness. 'I'm not supposed to be happy! If I am, I am getting away with it. It is my duty to suffer.' Now you may well think this is morbid, but just think of the situation that children today are born into, a long-standing inheritance of wrongs to be avenged, unhappiness as a duty.

So now it is time to tell the great story: of Jesus put to death by us and for us all and raised from the dead for us. Translation: our pain-body killed by us and transformed into a glorious body that we are all drawn into with baptism. The resurrection of the body of Jesus is the transformation of our pain-body into new life in God for ever. That's quite a translation, and there are some texts that are trying to say this – for instance, 'he was put to death *in weakness*, and raised *in strength*.' These texts are what Girard calls texts in travail, saying more than they could at the time because what they are about is timeless and for ever. Or texts in transition. Just think: Paul, who had been captivated on the Damascus road by Jesus risen, was able to speak of the body of this man he loved as 'our old man' that had to be destroyed to give birth to the new.

A simple way of putting all this is to say that what happened to the disciples of Jesus that Easter is the total transformation of humanity into a new life beyond the power and the fear of death. And it is given to our desperate age to know what total transformation feels like, what it entails in terms of our ordinary experience. And Tolle is not alone. Others, I know, have had the experience.

And here in conclusion is a dramatic account of something that happened to Tolle after the experience, one of his first experiences of 'passing it on'.[4]

> A woman in her thirties came to see me. As she greeted me, I could sense the pain behind her polite and superficial smile. She started telling me her story ... As a child she had been abused by a physically violent father. I saw quickly that her pain was not caused by her present life circumstances but by an extraordinarily heavy pain-body ...
>
> I directed her attention to what she was feeling inside her body and asked her to sense the emotion directly instead of through the filter of her unhappy thoughts, her unhappy story. She said she had come expecting me to show her the way out of her unhappiness, not into it. Reluctantly, however, she did what I asked her to do. Tears were rolling down her face, her whole body was shaking. 'At this moment, this is what you feel,' I said. 'There is nothing you can do about the fact that *at this moment* this is what you feel. Now, instead of wanting this moment to be different from the way it is, which adds more pain to the pain that is already there, is it possible for you to completely accept that this is what you feel right now?'... 'I am not asking you to *do* anything. All I'm asking is that you find out whether it is possible for you to allow those feelings to be there. In other words, and this may sound strange, if you don't mind being unhappy, what happens to the unhappiness? Don't you want to find out?'
>
> She looked puzzled briefly, and after a minute or so ... she said, 'This is weird. I'm still unhappy, but now there is space

around it. It seems to matter less.' This was the first time I heard somebody put it like that: there is space around my unhappiness. That space, of course, comes when there is inner acceptance of whatever you are experiencing in the present moment.

I didn't say much else, allowing her to be with the experience ... Another dimension had come into her life that transcended her personal past – the dimension of PRESENCE. Since you cannot be unhappy without an unhappy story, this was the end of her unhappiness. It was also the beginning of the end of her pain-body. Emotion in itself is not unhappiness. Only emotion plus an unhappy story is unhappiness.

For a Catholic Christian such as myself, the idea of the pain-body elucidates the doctrine of original sin with devastating clarity, for it is able to define the worst misinterpretation to which this doctrine is prone: that which takes the categorical imperative, 'Be unhappy!', to be the voice of God. I don't know of any theological definition of the error comparable to this.

2.5 Stretch into Love

The Tolle 'moment' of befriending the void and releasing the pain-body is nothing new – since Augustine, theologians, poets and philosophers have described the same experience in other ways. They agree that the void is not the end – it invites us into infinite love.

Mind-stretch

I want to think about six authors who are telling us the same thing about ourselves: that we stretch beyond ourselves – infinitely.

Take Tolle in his crucial night. He decides 'I cannot any longer live with myself.' A voice says 'that's odd. Are there two of me?' Then 'maybe only one of them is real', and this terrifies him and he lies there in bed shaking. He is experiencing our greatest fear, annihilation. He is holding on to himself against what he calls a vortex of energy pulling him in and down into a void. And then the voice says 'resist nothing!' which means 'stop insisting on yourself against what's coming, and let it come, just let go, totally!' He obeys, surrenders, and is filled with peace for the first time in his life, falls into a sleep out of which he awakes into a world of light in which he has lived ever since, teaching what he now knows.

Now take this statement of the poet Browning: 'a man's reach should exceed his grasp, / Or what's a heaven for?'[5] Isn't this what the Tolle moment is about? My reach is all the desire, all the longing in me, reaching out to infinity. My grasp is what I can hold onto now, me as I am now. So there is this urge *in* me beyond my contented present state. Surely there is a similarity between the force that Tolle feels in him which he wants to resist and the reach-beyond to which Browning refers. There is a big difference too: for Tolle the force is terrifying, for Browning it is merely reaching out, wanting always more. The difference is only in the intensity of the thrust within me out beyond me.

Now Augustine has a statement that is relevant here. He says to God, 'you have made us for yourself, and our heart is restless till it rests in you.'[6] He is referring to the same human fact, of reach beyond grasp; he's explaining it theologically, but it's the same human tension as in Tolle and Browning.

Amazingly it has only just occurred to me that a saying of mine that once came to me and proved useful for teaching, is saying the same thing: desire is love trying to happen; it's the same reach beyond myself that we all have in us. Love is the end, the goal, the consummation, and desire strains towards it, wants to be it.

And here is another witness, Bernard Lonergan SJ, who has taught me most of what I know about the mind and its ways. His most basic formula is that we are 'self-transcendent'. He builds a whole system on this, and it works because it is powerfully true.

Finally there is a thinker I have always been trying to understand: Maurice Blondel. He was a Catholic thinker who managed to get into the French philosophical world of the nineteenth century, which was militantly sceptical. He wrote a book called *L'Action*. We *have* to act, and action takes us beyond ourselves, it's such a dynamic idea that I've found it difficult, disconcerting, disturbing. His language is muscular. The big distinction he makes is between *la volonte voulue* and *la volonte voule*, between the will willed and the will willing – not 'willing' in the colloquial sense but in the sense of the act of will. Now what he is saying is that there is the will *in* me, impelling me ever further, and the will I exercise here and now and within my grasp. This is the same as in Browning's 'reach' and 'grasp'. We outreach our grasp ('Or what's a heaven for?' is Browning's chatty version of St Augustine).

So militant was the intelligentsia in Blondel's day that the word 'Action' does not appear in the philosophical dictionary. We have a lot to learn from this. Blondel was dealing with a complacent atheism, and unlike the church of the time that merely fulminated, he went to the human heart at its roots. I'm sure you won't be surprised to learn that his orthodoxy was suspect in the church.

So there we are; Tolle, Browning, Augustine, Moore, Lonergan, Blondel. I'm sure there are lots more, because it's the truth about us, whether writhing in terror in bed, anguishing with the desire to love and be loved, doing whatever it is I do, relentlessly thinking and banging on the door of official philosophy in its complacency.

As Tolle discovered, that it is *by invitation of the void* that we come into truth. As between the void that terrifies and repels, the void that terrifies and invites. We may learn from the Tolle experience that the void is friendly and in love with us, in a way that we are no longer learning this powerfully from the church, whose teaching on sexuality especially, and on us gays and lesbians more especially, is telling us little of this. Self-hatred is virulent in today's western culture of death, and the church is if anything reinforcing it.

2.6 Stay Awake

Embracing the void is prayer in the body, distanced from the pain-body but not disembodied. Christ invites the disciples at Gethsemani to watch and pray, to stay awake. To stay awake in the way Tolle suggests is to be aware of the divine within, to participate in God incarnate. This entails letting go – even of Christ, as he himself knew he had to die.

Make it simple, stupid!

What most people today who seriously believe in God are not getting from the churches to which they belong is what might be called a map of reality, the ultimate and the close-at-hand, showing the path from the latter to the former. A chart, or a method.

Such a chart is provided by Eckhart Tolle who, in a truly amazing experience, stumbled on ultimate reality on the point of committing suicide.

Now if it is possible to *have* that experience through carefully reading Tolle, then a person would have before him or her the mental charting of the unknown that we must be supremely desirous of. I am a very old monk, long-practised in the 'way in' opened by my tradition. But my life has been changed by Tolle. For even as a monk schooled for sixty years in Catholic theology, I came upon Tolle as my first 'map' of the type I am wishing for for all of us. But now I *know myself*, uncharted and yet undoubtedly existent, deprived of all my habitual landmarks, as the consciousness of the universe, the universe as conscious. It is only at this point that my faith as a Catholic Christian tells me that I am not identically God but am God by participation in the incarnate Son of God. The first thing my faith has to tell me is that I am not God while through the Tolle experience I know myself *in* God. My faith nuances this by saying I am God by adoption in a way that involves everything about me in the second, to-hand experience that is mine. That's a pretty hefty nuance!

Now I step back and begin to see how wretchedly impoverished would be my Catholic Christian consciousness were it not for Tolle's *natural*, secular opening of my inner door.

Tolle opens the door into a deep self that all the world religions are about and differ about. If you go by 'the light of Asia' of Buddhism and Hinduism, the deep self is identical with God. If you are a Christian, the deep self is God through Jesus who is in the 'second' world, of the to-hand, as well as in the first.

But in the world we live in today, it is of incomparably greater moment to know that we *have* a deep self than whether you believe in a Christian or a Buddhist or a Hindu way.

Christian–Buddhist dialogue

There is a well-known Buddhist saying, 'If you meet the Buddha on the road, kill him!' The meaning is, that the enthusiastic disciple comes to idolise the Buddha from whom he is learning to live; so, if you find yourself imagining, excitedly, your teacher, kill this image and go into the void, the loss of ego that he teaches in the great Fire Sermon.

Now with the disciple of Jesus, there is a different situation. For unlike the disciple of the Buddha, the disciple of Jesus has been taught that Jesus himself is the way. As this Pope's new book[7] makes clear, the message of Jesus is, 'You have heard it said of old, but I say …' The teaching finds its focus in the teacher. The disciple is encouraged, by the teacher, to pin his hopes on him, he is to follow him wherever he is going. And where is that? A horrible fiasco. Unlike the Buddha, who died in the normal way, Jesus was the victim of a lynch-death supported by the authorities of the time, priestly and secular.

Now let us set side by side the situation of the disciple of the Buddha and that of Jesus' disciple. The Buddha's disciple has never been encouraged to idolise him. And the instruction 'if you meet him, kill him!' is simply emphasising this non-centrality of the teacher. Jesus' disciple, on the other hand, has been encouraged to focus on the teacher, so that when the whole movement comes to this horrible end, there is every incentive to imagine Jesus as he was and pretend that the dreadful has not happened. It can't have!

So the centring of the disciple on the teacher is, in the case of the Buddha, something never encouraged, the discouragement playfully emphasised by the injunction to 'kill him', while in the case of Jesus it is something encouraged and then bitterly disappointed. The difference is, that the urge to focus on the leader, gently discouraged by the Buddha, is in the case of Jesus massively reinforced by the experience of bereavement that always and everywhere has the bereaved imagining it has not happened, and keeping the beloved alive with all the resources of imagination.

Now it is self-evident to the sceptic that this refusal to believe Jesus was dead is what found expression in the belief that he was 'risen'. There are serious objections to this suggestion, but they are not my present concern. My concern is to show that if Jesus did show himself to the disciples in a way that has given us a world-changing faith, this showing would have done something to their keeping Jesus alive that would have displaced it in favour of a new enlightenment with a Jesus nearly unrecognisable, the Jesus they had to proclaim as 'the firstborn of the dead'.

But the point is that this new enlightenment entailed a vigorous letting-go of the Jesus of imagination, what I call the ego's Jesus. Tolle says that one should not, in meditation, imagine Jesus, and Abbot Chapman says that when you are being carried by Jesus you don't see his face.

For me, Buddhism and Christianity are in harmony, in that both entail this huge letting-go of the ego and its whole world. For years, teachers like William Johnston SJ have been saying that Buddhism and Christianity do not compete, and it is only a fundamentalist Christianity that wants them to. Fundamentalism clings to the ego's Jesus and will not let him die for the real Jesus to rise in us and address a world in mortal anguish.

Jesus himself said he had to die, and saw his death as the dying of a seed to 'bear much fruit', and this theme pervades the last discourses in

John's Gospel. 'It is expedient for you that I go' – and this 'go' is not funeral parlour language – 'think of me as having gone into the next room.' It refers to a horrendous death, and implies that this is the dying that the world needs, the death of the universal scapegoat-victim of the violence that is now world-suicidal. There is a heavy human implication in the Johannine version of the necessary death of the Jesus-image. It is not only mystical. It is political.

But its shape is mystical, the shape is the transformation of the human by the more-than-human Spirit. It was said of Thomas Merton and the Dalai Lama after their conversation that they smiled like two cats that had shared a saucer of cream. Conversely, I am encouraged by the Buddhist monks in Burma protesting against that awful regime.

What do we mean by 'God' when we say that Buddhism does not have a God? We mean, presumably, a being we think of as not human and infinitely powerful. Buddhism does not have such a being in its system. It is human-centred.

But this God, that Buddhism is said not to have, we Christians do not have either. This is the God of which Dawkins writes, who fundamentalists say exists and he says doesn't. But there is no such God. More precisely, a God conceived of as 'another being', an entity over-against us, has been characterised by Le Senne as '*Dieu sans nous*',[8] about whom we can say things that are nothing do do with us. This is a travesty of the God in whom Christian faith believes.

To speak of God, we must remember that Jews are not allowed by their scriptures to speak his name; they have only the Tetragrammaton to refer to our total non-groundedness in ourselves. What we mean by God is the reminder that we are not the ground of our own being, that we are dependent on a reality that is totally incomprehensible.

2.7 Stripped Bare

These 'Void Stanzas', responding to James Alison's 'Befriending the vacuum: Receiving responsibility for an ecclesial spirituality',[9] encapsulate the image of Christ entering the void at Gethsemani, pointing towards his public 'letting go' on the following day.

> Jesus dare I look
> With you into the void
> Where all creation shook
> And forms are unalloyed.

Your Adam still to be
Before without our sin
And nothing you could see
For all things to be in.

In the Garden alone
The terror before time
At the newly unknown
Before creation's slime.

Now you your Father know
Unspeakably not yet
Out of nothing to grow
The huge to be, forget.

In this vertigo
Of your Gethsemani
The void where he would grow
To Spirit energy.

Creation here could be
Guessed at time as you prayed
Father and energy
Between them now displayed

The world entirely new
With love instead of death
That was to do with you
Secret under the breath

That picks me up in prayer
To resonate with you
Accomplished everywhere
Your Father's will come through

In a new-martyred world
A cloud of witnesses
Love's banner now unfurled
Where lovers all say yes.

Now in your darkest psalms
Of the body destroyed
The promise the heart warms
The flesh denied, destroyed.

Absolute still to be
The body sweating blood
Unable for the free
Abounding of the good

In hosts of saints to be
The fruit of your tomorrow
Born of Gethsemani
In unimagined sorrow.

O seen and nothing seen
The Father's not-yet will
Where nothing yet can mean
Depending on the kill.

And as I contemplate
Beginning, no before,
Perhaps I feel the weight
In you of something more,

The Father's will to be
Now is all gut and blood
In you we know as he
The new incarnate word.

Love strip me of the forms
Of life all readymade,
Expose me to the storms
Of which I am afraid

Out of which you are risen
Into the Spirit's wind
To free us from this prison
In a dead culture blind.

Your body stripped and scourged
The sanctuary degraded
Suddenly I am purged
My complacency raided.

The stripping of the forms
Done by the soldiery
And only now there storms
On me who will not see

Now think of me undressing
And of Jesus the same:
What am I now confessing,
Some comic cosmic shame

This blasphemy was needed
Of him undressed exposed
For his word to be heeded
And at last interposed.

Love stripped him of the clothing
Whereby we are disguised
And my confusion loathing
Body risen surprised.

My brothers as we are
In love, spirit creates
Makes unfamiliar
As prayer upon us waits.

O it was all done then
To eyes long since gone blind
To put all in a pen
Of rhetoric too kind.

Yet Paul knew to exult:
His lover in the flesh
Destroyed that would result
The Body Spirit fresh.

The muddled Catholic sex
In this fell melting-pot
Shall cease to be a hex
Of which we were begot

To later priestly shame
Now to the world exposed
For which we have to blame
The thing we interposed,

Into our young men trained
Womanless as a caste
With sex instilled ingrained
In lurid colours fast.

Now Spirit anew
Will blow across the scene
And what we always knew
Will look to us obscene

Until the purge has done
The stripping of the forms
Seen anew in the Son
Who undermines our norms

And draws all to himself
As he promised, foreknew
Sweeps from our Catholic shelf
Old lies to make us new.

That wants to tear my heart out
Of all from here the stripping
Now tear the ego's part out
The point of final tipping.

3

Friday Afternoon – Broken Body on the Cross

Christ crucified is a victim vindicated with love beyond
sacrifice, creating a dangerous memory by destabilising
existing power structures.
(René Girard[1] on overcoming violence)

*On Friday afternoon, the consequences of befriending the void at Gethsemani
are played out. Christ crucified meets self-punishment and dominance head on,
becoming the victim of our desires, taking the side of the part of us that wants to
love.*

*This interpretation of Christ's final sacrifice by René Girard, coupled with
Tolle's concept of the pain-body, together offer a challenge to Christians to look
hard at their understanding of desire and sin, sacrifice and salvation.*

*The death of Christ is the death of our pain-body, a new way of understanding
Paul's idea of being crucified 'in the flesh'. Christ on the cross is also the final
scapegoat, the priest and visible victim who exposes sacrifice as murder.*

*The cross still challenges us to love more fully. The church still has scapegoats,
as institutional homophobia shows, and still has a pain-body, as the abuse crisis
shows. The cross vindicates the victim, pointing the way from pain to love, from
death to life.*

3.1 Sin and Salvation: A Dangerous Memory

*Befriending the void, allowing the true self to emerge: Thursday night has
implications for our understanding of sin, sacrifice and salvation, as the events
of Friday afternoon show. Christ crucified becomes a willing victim, dissolving
the myth of dominance and self-punishment. The memory of this is powerful – it
is dangerous.*

With the experience and the concept of befriending the void, we have something new for salvation doctrine: a salvific experience we share with the Saviour. He befriends the void as our pioneer, which the Letter to the Hebrews describes him as. So it was at Gethsemani, perhaps, that the ego gave way totally to let in the true self for whom a horrible death was to be the final sacrifice, not as the at last successful bloody sacrifice satisfying a monstrous God, but as the reality of which the bloody victims of old religion are a foreshadowing travesty rather than a 'first attempt'.

By the solution I am suggesting, we can at last give a meaning to 'sacrifice' that remains, as recently remarked, the most treacherous word in the Christian vocabulary. This meaning is found in, if you like, a marriage with the void, a surrender in defiance of the body's protest in bloody sweat. This protest of the body is, in a recent bold translation, *Good As New*,[2] said to have taken place *in consequence* of Jesus' final acceptance.

Thus we can bring together, the Johannine statement, 'you do not take my life, I lay it down of myself', the image in Hebrews of Jesus as the pioneer of faith, and above all the concept of the death of Jesus as sacrifice, with all its misleading connotations needing the genius of Girard to unscramble.

Sacrifice for sin

The way we have to correct the story of our salvation from original sin is not – as I've always thought – by critiquing the story of the Fall and getting into the morass of myth versus reality. It is quite different. It is to come up with a good account of how salvation is experienced, of what salvation is experienced as, namely the liberation from an inveterate consciousness shaped by fear and guilt and self-hatred and self-punishment. For this takes us straight to Jesus, willing victim of a lynch-death as universal scapegoat who, risen from the dead, is all forgiveness and the radical undoing of our systems of guilt and its false remedies.

This is the dangerous memory of the prisoner who dissolved the myth of dominance, the original sin that history is under. Michel Foucault is illuminating here, when he points out that wherever you alight in history you find people who have power holding onto it, and people who lack power striving to obtain it. A moment of emancipation from this, the Jesus pivotal moment of Gethsemani, inserted in the faithful consciousness, has been aptly called a dangerous memory by

Johann Baptist Metz,[3] a great German theologian, disciple of Karl Rahner. It is dangerous to know that the whole system of this world can be, has been, subverted by the introduction of the Kingdom of God. This memory is indelibly registered in the annals of the prison that history is. Somehow the church has this dangerous memory whose nostalgia creates martyrs; the men and women to whom he showed himself risen from the dead, taking away their fear and filling them with the love of God.

The remedy for a theory of salvation based on an inherited sin and the need for its repairing is a taste of salvation itself as the emancipation from a state of self-punishment, itself regarded till that moment as 'a good thing', acting for God against one's sinful self.

The bad, inveterate formula is: I am ill at ease with myself. So the bad salvation formula is the theological elaboration of this self-hatred: that God agrees with my judgement on myself. But my self-hatred cannot be godly. So how does God figure, how does my self-evaluation expand into theology once I recognise that self-hatred is not a correct attitude to myself, untrue to me? What God is *then* seen to be doing is reinforcing the opposite of self-hatred, which is self-love. God is trying to persuade me to love myself *and thus* go against my whole upbringing as an inheritor of the idols of our culture, our gods whereby we idolise our social biases. In thus letting God in to my self-opposing psyche as peacemaker, I live in another universe, one ruled by love between people. Now this change in the account of what God is doing has a model, Jesus. Jesus lived, acted and taught, in what he called, lovingly and wistfully, the Kingdom, and this led to his crucifixion by the world that is not ruled by love but by the idols that model our self-hatred. Sacrifice to 'the prince of this world' is an act of self-destruction. For as Girard says, the scapegoat is killed not because he is unlike us but because he is like us, he represents the goodness in ourselves that we destroy. Human sacrifice is self-destruction to appease the gods of this world.

So it should be possible to contrast the true and the false formula. The false has God against us who are against ourselves. At the base is a human sacrifice, Jesus whom God destroys instead of us. On the cross, says Luther, God unleashes his fury at sin on his Son in our place. The true formula has God on the side of our goodness in the world, which means turning our back on the gods of this world who urge on our self-hatred, so that we 'feel the draught' of no longer being good in the way we were taught, no longer conforming to 'the ways of this world' as

Paul says. 'Little children, keep away from idols!' as old John writes. Idols regiment us to secure the world's violent order.

When we hear that we are sinners, and that God is seeking to cure us, we naturally assume that in condemning ourselves we are on the side of God against our sinful selves. Now this response, unfortunately, is in harmony with a quality of self-hatred that is in us already, so religion becomes divine reinforcement of our self-hatred.

So long ago that it is embarrassing to remember it, I was saying that God was trying to cure us of 'feeling bad about feeling good'. That was right. God is on the side, not of that in us which hates ourselves but, on the contrary, of a tender centre that wants to love, so that God who *is* love is going to be on the side of *that*, blowing on the feeble spark to bring it into the fire of love.

And once we understand this, we recall that the main thrust of Jesus' ministry was to do this very thing, of quickening the spark into flame, with the despised of society, the outcasts, the tax-collectors and the prostitutes. Society was doing to *them* what we do to *ourselves*, condemning on the side of God. We hate ourselves *in* ourselves and *in* the people who represent our sinfulness, the tax-collectors and the whores.

This befriending of the rejected and the weak was seen by Nietzsche as the essential flaw in Christianity, and this diagnosis by the most penetratingly introspective person should tell us something. The man who hated our weakness saw in Christ its strongest ally, and found himself in a tortured relationship with Jesus. In this madness he would sign his letters, 'the crucified'. So, to simplify: we are prone to self-hatred, and make victims to bear the brunt of this, build a system that requires victims and outcasts. *Religion* says God is on our side in this judgemental attitude. *Jesus* is on the side of the victims of our judgement, the self and the outcasts of the social self.

To follow Jesus is to be on the side of God whose sun shines on the just and the unjust alike. This is a most radical change of attitude. But it is a change that is the undoing of self-hatred, of self-punishment. It is learning to say, inwardly, deeply, as I look at the world, 'it's all right!' Religion says it's all wrong. I am slowly learning to say 'it's all right!' And *then* I find suddenly that that I am one with the power of now. I am getting myself into the draught of being 'all right' in myself, and to know the pain of *this!*

This may have some connection with the following insight of Ziziou-las, that

> there is the tragedy of our longing for a true personhood that we sense that we do not possess. When we recognize this

tragedy, we know that we cannot transpose our concept of person to the being of God. It is the reverse of what we should do, namely allow God's way of being to reveal true person-hood.[4]

Perhaps Jesus does this, and lets us into his moment of freedom, baptised into his death for life in God.

3.2 Pain-Body Crucified

The death of Christ is the death of our self-hatred, of our pain-body. This sheds new light on Paul's theme of being crucified 'in the flesh' – the world's pain-body is destroyed to liberate it into love.

Every Easter is different

Does not the ego's Jesus have to die
If he is to be all he is in me
And so I have to want to crucify
And with his gathered murderers agree.

He called on two disciples to assent[5]
To his death at the hands of sinful men:
The transformation of our will's intent
Is violent, as crucifixion then.

The violence that grace does to the soul
Which, mortal, is fast-wedded to self-will
Kills Jesus, who surrendered his life whole
And shed humanity God's void to fill.

To be misunderstood could be my bliss
Admission of the everlasting kiss.

Or

And certainly I must be violent
With ego so inalienably bent.

I am trying to deal with the problem set by Paul when he says we have to crucify the flesh (the ego of course, not what we today mean by the flesh). I mean, that we have to renounce, and vigorously, our ego. But why does Paul use for this vigorous action the word for what they did to Jesus? Perhaps the answer is that in this life, in life as we know it, the ego is alive and well, and has to be, and self-esteem is a good and necessary thing. So life *wholly* beyond the ego has to be life beyond life as we know it; so Jesus, the model of life beyond the ego, had to die to become all that he is and show himself to draw us on.

The Great Story with the help of Eckhart Tolle

Let us start at a different place. Let us say that there is a tendency in us that seems inborn, strong in some, less so in others, stronger in some nations and cultures than in others, a tendency that is a felt duty or obligation to be unhappy and to spread unhappiness in the cause of righting some wrong. It is an unhappiness inherited to be passed on. And Girard comes in here, for this tendency, that Tolle calls the pain-body, looks very like desire mimetically charged which, though it is love trying to happen, opens up avenues of rivalry, tying us up in intractable knots of desire. This is only a more grounded and sophisticated way of referring to the bending of desire toward suffering and unhappiness which Tolle refers to as the pain-body. What, then, would the radical cure of this condition look like? It would look like the eradication of this universal death-wish (not a bad word for the pain-body).

Now look at the Jesus story, the story of a great prophet who proclaimed a big change that was soon to come, a radical change. Like any prophet he soon became a leader who said something different from other leaders. He said, 'Follow me!' Whither? Stay with me and you'll see, and in the end want to come with me. And this leader put God on the spot. He said that the new age he was bringing in was the reign of love to displace the reign of, well, the pain-body, the perpetual misery and cruelty of this world.

How, just how, was he to bring about the transformation of the pain-body into what the body is about: love, the body we all are and are in? But the next thing we learn is that this man was put to death by all that goes into the pain-body, all the disappointed expectations converging on him in the history he was part of. At this stage, tantalisingly, the body of Jesus becomes the victim of the situation he creates by his challenge of all that goes into the order, the fear-constituted order of the world, the reign of death. So Jesus is laden with the gravity of the pain-body that drags down the world.

Then, after his execution, he returns and rallies his disconsolate followers, and when they see him and he explains all, their heart burns within them. And out of this experience comes the conviction that the reign of God *has* come, its centre the mysterious life-giving risen Body of the victim. So this man's violent death, issuing in the rallying love of one another beyond the power of death, has brought about the reign of love in this world.

But this immediately puts up the question: how? And theologians have wrestled with this question ever since. So how has that death changed the world for ever?

For answer, we must go to Paul. The deepest and most adventurous promoter of the new faith has dared to say that the body of Jesus, loved by his followers and erotically loved by Mary Magdalen, was 'our old self' and had to die for us to be reborn. What a way to talk about someone he was in love with since his experience on the Damascus road! But, confidently and fearlessly, Paul did. Captivated by the risen Jesus, Paul was able to see the earthly Jesus as embodying the old self that had to be destroyed to let the Spirit bring us to eternal life in God. After all, the whole story climaxes with him being killed, his body destroyed. What is shocking is the positive meaning given to this destruction in the larger perspective of Paul.

Now try to assemble the picture. Remember that we have already seen that our need is for the eradication in us of the duty of sadness by its opposite, the bliss of the one who displaces it, the contagion of happiness coming upon us wilful sufferers. The displacement of this ill will by the bliss of God is, we have seen, what our cure had to consist in. And now we recall the message at its most challenging, from Paul: the body of Jesus is our old self that has to be destroyed, so Jesus is killed. What saves this conclusion from the barbarity implied in saying that God required the killing of Jesus for his purpose, is not the reality of the pain-body that was killed in the person of Jesus. What I am suggesting is that the notion of the pain-body mediates between the acceptable fact that Jesus was killed and the problematic reason why he had to be killed. It gives me something I can feel.

The storm finds its eye in the man who is to offer himself on a cross 'with the joy ahead despising the shame', whose body is to become, in crisis, our pain-body. We are not quite done yet. Our pain-body is extinguished in the void, as happened to Tolle, as one man's experience. Jesus enters the void at Gethsemani. The body that sweated blood was the body to be destroyed – for who can doubt that the body was destroyed, killed, made dead? He took into the garden all the felt wrongs of humanity, where 'the curses against you fell on me' (Psalm 69:9b and Romans 15:3b).

And what of him, the leader? This brings us to the heart of the story, the story on the inside. What we have seen so far is the outside; we have confronted the paradox that he is the world's pain-body, whose destruction is our liberation from the pain-body into love. Now we move from this outside of the story, with its paradox of 'God wanted that body destroyed.' On the inside, the leader is, as the Letter to the Hebrews says, the pioneer of a new consciousness, made luminous in the moment of Tolle's crucial change.

3.3 Victim of our Desire

Christ is the loving victim of our desire, and on the cross he draws our desires towards himself, mediating and transforming them. This sacrifice becomes a sacrament of embodied love: the Eucharist.

Desire and the love of God

As I look back along a long life, I find that most of it that is given to thinking has one predominant theme: desire. Almost obsessively, I keep coming back to this. Now by far the most important thing about this concentration has been its deepening and enrichment by the insight into desire which has led René Girard to effect a Copernican revolution in literary criticism and, further, anthropology. But it is only lately that I have gone back to the book in which he first mined this insight as Professor of French Literature at Stanford University in the United States.[6]

René Girard has hypothesised that with the emergence of man from the animal, instinct is succeeded by desire, and desire is, through and through and from its very beginning in the embryo, imitative. Mirror-neurons appear in the foetus from the very start. As early as we wanted anything, we felt others wanting it, the breast for instance. And this is what has to be got into our diagram, so that the straight line between desirer and desired becomes the base of a triangle, of which the apex is the 'mediator' between the desirer and the desired. Whatever, or whom-ever, I want, others want, and it is much more difficult than we might imagine to say how much is me wanting and how much the imagined other wanting in me. Desire is mimetic, imitative, through and through. Here is the splendid statement of Girard:

> Denial of God does not eliminate transcendency but diverts it from the *au-delà* to the *en-deçà*. The imitation of Christ becomes the imitation of one's neighbour. The surge of pride breaks against the humanity of the mediator, and the result of this conflict is hatred.[7]

What I have said makes me suspicious of any claim to such a feeling. It took me some time to realise that for Girard 'metaphysical desire' is probably an instance of thinking of desire as my own, where it is 'mediated' by others' desires at the apex of our triangle. Are all my desires mediated to me in this way? Am I just at the point of interaction of the multiple traffic of desires? Or is there a 'stabiliser'? What would a stabiliser be like? A policeman? No, for a policeman is not a desiring one. He is external to the confusion he controls. The stabiliser must have attractive, inspiring qualities, and here I note that attraction has a vital role in the Girardian system, since it comes from *admiration* which is one prong of mimetic desire, the other being rivalry and envy.

When I realise that I *am* this convergence of desires and that what I call my desires are echoing desire in others, that is the first step of my present enquiry, where I stop and ask: is this situation all that there is to desire? One answer will be to ask: can I name a desire that is overwhelmingly my own, what I want above all? Ignatius in his Exercises has me name *id quod volo*, what I want, and this is obviously good spiritual direction. It's the question Jesus asks the two disciples at the start of his ministry in John's Gospel.

Now let's look again at this 'higher other', this exemplar at the apex of the triangle. Just suppose it is the record of a life such as ours, but drawing to itself as violence and love all the desires that converge on my desire, all the desire in us concentrated on a loving victim, his life culminating in murder and then through death transformed into love itself in a new human life that the hearts of disciples burned on recognising. Note too that *this* model not only transcends the desires that are the traffic at the apex. It *accepts* them as his crucifiers. Quite simply, it's one hell of a story.

3.4 Sacrifice Exposed as Murder

Christ's broken body is the body of a victim made visible – he exposes sacrifice as murder, opening it up to the forgiving love of God.

See, I make all things new

The victim of our cult, disposable,
Says of his body, tortured and destroyed,
'My body', breaks the sacrificial rule
In our one rite that no one may avoid.

How did he break the rule? With the word 'my':
How did he say it? Over broken bread –
Can you not see, do you not have to cry
Out against holy mutterings instead

Of his pellucid action? The shared meal
Articulates his torn and tortured flesh
In food and drink he dares to call our real
And gives us in a world deathless and fresh.

Our sacrifice this priest stood on its head
And did so in the breaking of the bread.

The first thing I learned from René Girard about human sacrifice was that the humanity of the victim has to be concealed. Iphigenia has to be blindfolded lest the people see her eyes, and the same is done with the victim of a firing squad. Jesus breaks this fundamental rule, in saying '*my* Body for you!' When I understood this, the Letter to the Hebrews came alive for me and I knew why I loved the words 'Christ the High Priest of the things to come'. The priesthood of this victim makes all things new, it isn't just a charming theological conceit.

I like to think of Girard as the Hercule Poirot of theology. Here are all the suspects ruminating on the Sacred Passion, and here is Poirot asking: 'Who did it, does it, and continues to do it, and why?'

Reflections on the Christian sacrifice

There is a powerful force in our theology that pulls *away* from the vivid focus in the sacred *convivium*.[8] This is the word sacrifice, acknowledged at last as the most treacherous word in the Christian vocabulary. But surely, it will be urged, the Paschal Lamb, with all its connotations of human sacrifice and its animal substitute, draws attention to itself not as a seduction but as a luminous reality. This brings us to the heart of the matter, which is, that the new *convivium* of Jesus renders obsolete the old world of a god or gods appeased by bloodshed. The great event that ends all this is the world-approved murder of the Son of God, who declares a new covenant 'in *my* blood'. This obsolescing of bloody sacrifice is the theme of the Letter to the Hebrews, and when this Letter does have blood calling on God, it is not that of the sacrificial victim but of our murdered brother Abel.

This counter-attraction of old bloody sacrifice has bedevilled our theology, and one name stands out, above all others, as defusing it, that of René Girard, who defuses it by exposing it as shared murder in disguise. Grasp this, and the wind is taken out of old sails, or, to change the metaphor, the air escapes from the inflatable toy of the religious, security-seeking ego.

Calvary exposes as murder what was for the powers that be a religious sacrifice of a trouble-maker, prescribed by Caiaphas the High Priest. This exposure opens our murder of the Son to the forgiving love of God, which puts an end to an age-old history of bloody sacrifice, human and, by replacement, animal. Words fail us as we attempt to enter the mind of Jesus on entering the agelong human charade. Of the human condition as needing Jesus to save it, I am suddenly reminded of the epigraph to that disturbing book, *We Need to Talk About Kevin*.[9] 'Where a child needs love most, he deserves it least.' Paul, in love with Jesus since his devastating experience, says that for a good man someone might die, but God's love appears in this, that while we were still his enemies Christ died for us.

There is an awful implication in an insufficiently worked-out theory about this crucial event. It is that the murder deemed a sacrifice is made to *be* a sacrifice by reason of the Godhead of the victim. In a flourish to sell this lie, it is pointed out that *this* victim is priest as well, and thus offers to God his own body as an acceptable sacrifice. What kind of God would do that?

We must notice above all what is kept intact by this theory, the sacrificial value of a man put to death. Not only does this sacrifice have divine value by means of the divinity of the victim. By a perverse twist of the mind, it occupies the whole scene, and makes the Resurrection superfluous, icing on the cake, whereas it is the Resurrection *alone* that discloses the victim to his bewildered and joyful disciples as the bearer of divine vindication extended to all the victims of history. What the risen victim does to his disciples who are to become church is to show up his 'sacrifice' as murder by a state-empowered lynch-mob, which is thus shown as forgiven in a baptism that totally transforms. The forgiveness of all sins in Baptism, self-evident to the church from her birth, is bestowed in the appearing of the victim at the sight and discourse of whom the heart burns, as recorded in Luke's account of the road to Emmaus.

The way the word sacrifice behaves in the wretched account of a theology that became conventional is what has led a perceptive theologian to describe it as the most treacherous word in the Christian vocabulary. The divinity of the victim, far from conferring sacrificial status on Calvary, dissolves it.

This revisionary transformation of the word sacrifice makes the *true* sacrifice our food *before* Jesus identifies the bread as his body. It creates for us a newly symbolised reality, 'the bread of life'. 'The bread of life' – who ever heard of that? – nourishes something new in us, the true self evoked by the vindicated, non-vindictive and forgiving victim impressing on the soul of the disciple the risen condition of having died into life beyond life. Jesus feeds the soul not metaphorically but by bestowing the food that 'the eternal in man' – to quote Scheler[10] – needs. This rooting of the Eucharistic meal in the emancipation from sacrificial religion is conveyed by the liturgy properly performed and understood, that shows its nourishing character from the very start of the ritual. There is, it now occurs to me, a close connection between 'nourishing' in this context and 'flourishing', leading to a theology of divine abundance massively replacing the stingy exacting God that we have let into the Christian mind through that awful initial mistake, of invoking the divinity of the victim to validate spiritually our murder in its perennial sacrificial disguise.

3.5 Scapegoats Still

Christ is the scapegoat on Friday afternoon – we still have scapegoats, as does the church. Homophobia is a contemporary example. A broader sacramental understanding of love can challenge this.

> In keeping Jesus up there on the cross
> Resolutely we resist his resurrection

Because we cannot stand the only loss
We need, to come under his high direction.

Paul tells us that we have to crucify
Him still, but this is not what we are doing
Endlessly to prolong the agony
Keep him alive for our continual ruining.

When he was dead they took him off the cross
But when we keep him on it for our prayer
We're not with Paul who took a fearful toss
Into the nothing that is everywhere.

To keep him crucified, to let him die
Are opposites for wisdom from on high.

The word of Paul was single: Crucify!
He meant the old man, not the other man,
The me I hate because I will not try:
He meant the ego, and all that I can.

The church has taken the wrong turning here
With savage persecution of the Jews
Or of the body bullied under prayer:
There is the road less travelled we may choose

In which it is the ego that we kill,
Its dreams projected on the paschal lamb
The victim who continually keeps still
Only to rise, eternal love I AM.

Here is what Paul originally meant:
Do him to death and end self-punishment.

The way I was brought up, as a Catholic boy, to think about 'the Jews'
was certainly supplying the soil in which the Nazi anti-Semitism took
root. And this certainly affects the spirituality I was brought up on. It is
an 'anti' attitude to life. Sixty years ago, I was calling it a Catholic
neurosis, the title of an article that gave rise to episcopal fury and the

attempt to get me removed from the parish on which I was serving. It makes me happy to think that this at least is being named and eschewed. Of course there are other 'bad attitudes' that have still to reveal themselves. How about the official teaching that homosexuality is 'a deviance'? The point is that being a Catholic does not guarantee a good attitude to life. We have to pray for it.

Girard says we all scapegoat, and adds, 'I don't know who my scapegoats are.'

On the collapse of the homosexual taboo

Our civilisation is breaking in on institutional Christianity with the shedding of its oldest taboo. The reactions have been in character, the Anglican chaotic, the Catholic impassive, neither of them pastorally helpful to the persons in question, who in fact are sacrificed. Ratiocination toward human flourishing emphatically refuses to describe homosexuals as defectively human. But what they do, according to the taboo still in place, is a travesty of the union of man and woman. This travesty, the Pope is urging, is humanly self-destructive, comparable to the tearing down of our rainforests. But how? Well, the action is not destructive, it is simply alternative. So it has to be the people who do it who constitute a virus in society. They are a virus because they are defectively human. This category is unavoidable by anyone who is seeing the taboo not as the enslavement of certain people but as the upholding of the integrity of society. So while the taboo is being overtly deplored, it is kept in effect by statements of a grandiose nature about the integrity of society threatened with self-destruction by these people and what they do. And they are censured by a language that never mentions them, but implies them as dedicated to the destruction of humanity. And what does ratiocination toward human flourishing make of such a force, such a counter-flourishing?

Imposing the man–woman relationship as normative is maintaining the taboo in magisterial disguise. That word 'normative', of course, is flexible: at one end, it can mean simply sex for the vast majority. At the other end, it lets into itself the world 'ought'. But in between is the existential reality of male and female. Nicholas Lash wants to allow, for the middle existential area, the notion of 'privilege'. The church privileges the man–woman relationship as, simply, the sacrament of marriage, and surely that's straight -!- theology. It is when this 'privilege' takes on a 'to be preferred' quality, that the taboo reinserts itself and poisons the magisterium.

The term homophobia is now common. I do not hesitate to say that it describes the unavowed attitude of Catholic authorities to same-sex relationships. An outstanding example of this is Pope Benedict. I would instance two examples. As Prefect of the CDF, his treatment of the New Ways Ministry was one which Paul Collins (an Australian Catholic writer on religious issues) found it impossible not to describe as vicious. Benedict is a highly intelligent and well-informed theologian. He certainly knows that the official teaching that homosexuality is a 'disorder' is problematic, and that homosexuality has been struck off the list of deviances by the Psychiatric Associations of this country and America. The Catechism is very cautious in describing the official position – it starts by admitting that we do not know the cause of homosexuality and that it is not chosen. Yet he could impose on the New Ways Ministry as the condition of any acceptance as a pastoral initiative, that each of the two founders sign a statement, 'with mind and heart I acknowledge that homosexuality is a disorder.' The emphatic nature of the requirement goes far beyond the Catechism's language.

Far more striking is my second example. In the early days of the Anglican controversy over homosexual clergy, Cardinal Ratzinger went out of his way publicly to associate the Catholic Church with the evangelical wing of the Anglican controversy, who were against homosexual clergy. Theologically this was astonishing. Archbishop Rowan Williams is making the most acute and helpful distinction between first- and second-order theological problems. To the latter pertain all the questions to do with gender and sexual conduct among the clergy. Homosexuality as a clerical problem is second-order. Yet here was the official Catholic expert in dogmatic teaching accepting by implication the intrusion of second-order problems into a first-order ecclesial debate. This intrusion was, to my certain knowledge, severely censured by Cardinal Kasper, the head of the Unity department of the Vatican. Surely only the special homophobia that I am trying to get the measure of can account for it.

Cri de coeur

When the question of birth control came up at Vatican II and the Pope took it off the floor and gave it to an ad hoc commission, there came at last to a crisis the greatest anomaly there has ever been, surely, in the history of the church: that church pronouncements on sexuality have consisted, from the beginning, in the monitoring of sexual experience in those who have it by those who aren't supposed to. This is all documented, sometimes hilariously, in *Eunuchs for the Kingdom of Heaven*, by Ute Ranke-Heinemann.[11] The most dramatic effect of this anomaly was that the ecstatic joining of lovers in the con-fusion of orgasm was not what in fact it is, the occasion for the deepest thankfulness to our creator who is love itself, but a problem for the celibate mind that saw in it a suspension of reason. I still remember vividly the sense of shame engendered in a dogmatic theology class in Rome just after the war, at the mention of Dom Herbert Doms OSB, who had disgraced the Benedictine order by teaching that sexual pleasure had a vital role in marriage.

Thus it was the experienced reality of the act of love that was at last demanding recognition by a magisterium that had hitherto eschewed it. So it was an enormous learning moment for the teaching church.

This challenge was reinforced by an innovation of signal importance: planned parenthood, which the church was coming to accept. With this accepted, and the act of love pressing its claim against some two millennia of resistance, what was to be said about contraception?

The reasonable answer, surely, was that as long as children were not systematically excluded from a marriage, its use was permissible. And a few years ago, at the start of this pontificate, the Pope said to a group of married couples that it would be against love *systematically* to exclude children from a marriage. James Alison drew my attention to that adverb, and no one else seems to have noticed it; still it describes a marriage policy envisaged by the advocates of change – I remember 'une fécondité généreuse' as one of the chosen phrases. So what you had was a new situation in which sexual love was at last centre stage, and pregnancy could sometimes appropriately be called a risk.

But then occurred a theological intervention of incalculable moment. Theologian Karol Wojtyła, soon to be John Paul II, brought about a tour de force. For the opponents of change, he snatched victory from the jaws of defeat by saying that, far from pregnancy being a possible risk in a marriage, the openness to possible pregnancy was essential to the act of love itself. The spouses could not give themselves totally to each other *without* risking pregnancy! The victory was of the clerical over the lay! Once again the celibate understanding of sexuality was taking control and reversing the restoration of sexual love to its centrality in marriage.

Nor does the matter stop there. For this move of the Pope ties sexual love to procreation radically and organically, so that when the question of homosexuality comes up, the magisterium finds itself in the strong position of saying that a sexual union that *cannot* procreate is clearly a distorted one. No need now for the dubious use of the language of 'disorder', hurriedly explained as Aristotelian, not modern. So the crisis of sexual union, as viewed by the people concerned and not by celibates, shifts its centre of gravity from the married to gays and lesbians, with the good result of creating solidarity between them and the married, a solidarity, you could say, of civilised beings still challenging the teaching of the church. How long, O Lord, how long?

3.6 Pain-body still

The pain-body died with Christ on Friday afternoon – but the church still faces the challenge of its own pain-body in need of transformation, as the abuse crisis shows.

The Pope has just written a very moving letter to the Irish victims of child abuse. Somehow this has not got through. Is it that victims are never satisfied and always want more?

I don't think so. Something else is involved here. If we consult the experience of victims who have gone in distress to the official concerned, it is *what they then met* that sent a message that is absolutely chilling: of the system protecting itself against the victim. The Pope is not touching the experience that the victims have had, to which I am now referring. Here are some haunting examples. I know a man now in middle age and very intelligent. When he was a boy at a school run by religious brothers, a member of the community offended with one of the boys. What this man still remembers and still does not like to recall it, is how, when the thing got out, the priests 'closed ranks' against the boys who were themselves made to feel defiled. What this man still has 'raw' in his memory is the experience, shared with other boys, of implicit defilement communicated by the system as it preserved itself against its victim. Another case that I cannot forget is the story of a young American student in a Catholic university who was seduced for a long time by a brilliant young priest on the staff. Eventually he summoned up the courage to tell a priest on the staff, and – the same thing: the awful look in the eyes.

It is this *face* of the church, met with by the victim seeking help, that is indelibly inscribed in my memory, though I am not involved. There's something very powerful here. My guess – and it *is* only a guess, though one that haunts me – is that what the victim seeking comfort runs into is the dark side of the male celibate caste that rules over the Catholic

Church worldwide. What is this dark side? Tolle has a word for it; he calls it the pain-body, and defines it as an inherited addiction to unhappiness. I know it well as an inherent proclivity to self-punishment.

Now let us examine the priestly condition of living under mandatory celibacy. The man knows what he is undertaking, and this may be with passionate conviction to spread the love that God is in the world. Thus the sex-urge in him will be finding its fulfilment in love. But as celibacy is mandatory, there is at least the possibility that this most passionate of our urges will not be fulfilled, with celibacy maintained only by an act of the will. So you will have a condition of unfulfilment endured rather than sublimated. At this point, an inner voice will mutter, 'Well, what d'you expect? Life *is* about unfulfilment, pretty grim.' And this is the voice of the pain-body, feeding itself with a scrumptious ecclesiastical story. It is the voice that is making itself heard wherever celibacy is experienced as commanded not loved. The pain-body feeds on a loveless celibacy.

The copious work of Richard Sipe and Eugen Drewermann exploring this crisis of mandatory celibacy needs to be recalled at this critical time. Sipe has suggested that only 4 to 5 per cent of products of our seminaries achieve a celibacy that is the salt of the earth, the kind of men in whom Bonhoeffer saw the gospel personified, while 30 per cent keep their celibacy at the cost of remaining adolescent. Drewermann's enormous book[12] sees the system as producing 'shamans' en masse, equipped with an institutional conscience bound to loyalty to the system. He was severely punished for the book, I don't remember the details but they were close to laicisation. In any case, he has subsequently left the priesthood and the church.

Heroic efforts, I know, are being made in some seminaries to provide a fully human formation, and whether this is a losing battle certainly is not for me to say. I want to keep thinking about this clerical version of the deep dark thing in us, in me very strongly, bent as I am on self-punishment. Priests who mature beyond it are the salt of the earth, humorous, compassionate and life-enhancing.

Relevant, too, I think, is the tenacity with which the priesthood is wedded to celibacy. Although for the secular priest this is not vowed, only promised, it is taken much more seriously, when dispensation is sought, than monastic solemn vows, dispensation from which is easily obtained, whereas for secular priests only with the greatest difficulty. As regards a person being allowed to *return* to the priesthood once left, the rule is very serious – as we used to say, 'sacerdos numquam!' the bond being not that of a way of life, as with monks and nuns and so forth, but of an elite. And as Drewermann pointed out, this lays a patina of its elite-loyalty over a man's natural moral conscience. The effect is schiz-oid, and *into* the schizoid mind the pain-body with its negative message easily inserts itself.

How hard it is, against what hazards, to come to maturity! This is to bring the pain-body into a process of transformation. I am riveted by the thought that Paul was so captivated by the risen Jesus that he could refer to the Jesus that the disciples had known as a charismatic *person*, could see him in the larger dimension as 'our old man' who had to be killed for the new, the firstborn of the dead, to give himself to an astonished world. Paul says, 'our old man is crucified.' Try 'our pain-body is transformed'; a celibate male elite is going to have a joyless quality, and joylessness is the rule of the pain-body.

3.7 Victim Vindicated

Christ, the victim vindicated in love, shows us the way through pain to love, from death to new life, to freedom from vindictiveness; this is our challenge and our hope.

A new litany of the cross
In the cross is looking again at your neighbour in hope.
In the cross is the 'Tolle moment' of falling into the void
    resisting nothing.
In the cross is dissatisfaction with the status quo at the
    awakening of new possibilities.
In the cross shines Jesus the non-vindictive vindicated victim as
    my prayer model if I am a minority.
In the cross is a human future where everything human spells
    hopelessness.
In the cross is the risk of love.
In the cross is emancipation from routine and its enslavement.
In the cross is a partner seen as a new chance for love.
In the cross is the possibility to love again.
In the cross is our liberation from all the oppressions to which
    we are prone.
In the cross is tolerance, the overcoming of intolerance.
In the cross is the huge chance of God.

In the cross is victimhood vindicated and freed of
vindictiveness.

In the cross is victimhood not arrested at vindication.

In the cross is the oppression of a people suffered in a way of
solidarity and change.

In the cross the immemorial oppression of women is suffered in
a solidarity of liberation.

In the cross is life in suffering that otherwise perpetuates the
reign of death.

In the cross is the whole transit of people through pain into
solidarity and love.

In the cross is the story of Jesus happening again toward its
joyous outcome.

In the cross is silence in prayer and the chance of falling into
the void where all forms are born.

In the cross Jesus meets with the Buddha as desire is silenced
into love.

In the cross Islam, long feared by the church but drawn to Jesus
and Mary, is reconciled.

To the cross Jewry, whose persecution is the church's deepest
shame, is invited beyond vindication into the fraternity of
God.

In the cross is all the victimhood that ever was, vindicated and
freed of all resentment.

In the cross is the Transfiguration, vision of a new heaven and a
new earth.

In the cross is Apocalypse Now and for ever.

In the cross is Christian tyranny undermined.

In the cross is all suffering become unvengeful and
transforming.

In the cross is enmity become the love of the enemy.

In the cross is the whole trajectory of the human, the drama of
desire resolved in God its author.

In the cross is the death of the Lord remembered as long as
there is time, in the conviviality of the church.

In the cross is my suffering as God's opportunity.

In the cross is the festive abrogation of rivalry, the social
miracle.

In the cross is new light seen in the eyes of enemies.

In the cross I see as suffering what I just took for life.

The cross is set up as Jesus answers yes to the question of the
High Priest, are you the Son: on the cross, God passes
judgement on religion.
On the cross is Gaia, our earth mother, in this terrible end time.

4

Saturday Night – The Tomb in the Garden

Christ goes through death to pass beyond it, changing
death forever. We too are challenged to let go of our 'ego
Christ', letting him die in us so he can rise.
(Hengel and Hurtado's 'nuclear explosion[1])

*The tomb on Saturday is where everything seems to stop – Christ has let go,
nothing is happening, it's all over. Yet in the absence and emptiness, a new
presence is being forged.*

*Just as Christ was, when laid in the tomb, the dead are in a process of
transformation, becoming their true selves. This is more than an empty absence
or a pause before returning to the old way of living.*

*Christ is dead and buried. Facing the violent reality of Christ's death also means
facing our own end, and our capacity for self-destructive violence. Only when
they have seen him dead, and died to themselves, can the disciples see Christ
alive.*

*The empty tomb shatters our consciousness, like a nuclear explosion – death is
no more, and this means we have to live differently. Faith in the risen Christ is a
change of heart, a realisation that we are loved beyond imagining.*

4.1 Let Go of Ego: An Exercise in Presence

*On Friday afternoon, Christ lets go totally, even unto death. On Saturday, he
lies in the tomb, seeming absent, entering the unknown. Yet we fear his – and
our – presence, as much as the absence. In prayer, we can sink into the absence
that we so fear, and find God present.*

'Take up your cross', Ricoeur says, has an intellectual as well as a moral
meaning. Indeed it has for me. I have a voracious need to know, to

understand, to master. This is the ego's need to have power – over the God who surrendered all power into our murderous hands.

An experiment with the body

Most people have something about their body they don't like. And all our look-good magazines these days, male and female, reinforce this self-dislike: my body, I think, is misshapen and I don't like this, maybe I even hate it.

Now here's an experiment that you could try. I've learned at last, from Tolle, to do it with myself. It goes something like this: what I don't like about myself when I look at me in the mirror is X. Elaborate on this, go on and on about it. Then stop all that, stop the stories about yourself, how you were laughed at perhaps, and focus on 'me unhappy with the way I am'. It'll seem silly at first, but give it a chance: here I am, unhappy with me. You may find that there is space around this me-unhappy-with-me. It doesn't matter if this doesn't happen, it may happen another time – the mind has its own funny ways. But if you find there *is* space around you-unhappy, it may be that something else is coming in, something that Tolle calls Presence – big P! In this Presence, how you feel about yourself changes: in a way it's not important. We all get absolutely bogged down in the stories we tell ourselves, mostly not-good stories, and this stops us *living fully*.

What is my fear?

Jesus for me, face to face with my fear
Where I can pray me quietly in you,
I never feared that there was nothing there
Since you came to me so entirely new.

Annihilation, do I fear that?
Yes sometimes, when I fear to fall asleep
But as I pray, that's not where I am at:
What is the way you showed into the deep?

Is it of losing me or losing you?
Tough question that, it has me at a loss
Entering which I feel myself anew
In you my eros raised up on a cross,

And there you bring me to a deeper fear
Of my own world at having you too near.

I do not act out of the God I'm in
That is closer to me than I to me
And this is what we really mean by sin
As a condition, not activity.

Thus praying is to sink in all the way
To absolutely nothing in the mind
So that to breathe is really to pray
The certainty of 'seek and you shall find.'

This is the Jesus of the parables
And the whole style of him contagious
That undermines all the opposing wills
That come against him, so incurious.

Beware, religion, of an elsewhere God
Easily thought of, his extent the rod.

You were a happiness that I was in
And I gave way to this in layer by layer
Of anti-happiness that we call sin:
In other words, I came on inner prayer.

And then I wanted to read all about it
This inner bliss the theme of other souls
And what I read I understood, it shouted
At deaf confusion in holy roles.

A drawn-out love-affair with the unknown
Has been a beginning and of course no end,
One seed found soil wherein it could be sown
Grows heavenwards against the ego's bend.

Dying to self is partially successful
And happens, God knows how, in life all-stressful.

4.2 De Mortuis

Like Christ laid in the tomb, the dead are in a process of transformation, becoming their true selves. So life after death changes how we view the dead; Christ's fully human death also shows us how the dead are and what they will become.

There is life after death in this life. What is now surprising me is that I never thought of this as having implications for how we think of death and of the dead. Of course there is an implication about my death, but this is not a challenging one. Presumably death will find me shorn of the ego and its multiple ties of concern, as described in the first of the Duino Elegies of Rilke. But much more challenging is what 'the paschal break-through' implies for the way we think of the dead.

The state of the dead, we believe in our stated formula, is modelled on the risen Jesus. As he died and rose to life in God, so we in Baptism do. The reason why this formula sounds so convenient and perfunctory is that it is quite without interiority.

We have to apply to the dead what we say about Jesus, 'the pioneer of our faith'. And what we have to say about Jesus is that, risen, he is who he really is. Similarly, then, the dead are to be thought of as 'now who they truly are', a reality far beyond the person we came to know and love. Some French mystical type of writer quoted to me said that Jesus was the only wholly someone! And it does make sense to think of the life after death of our pioneer of faith as a sort of absolute of the person's becoming all of himself after death. Do we have here a superhuman 'I' that is 'of the Father in the Spirit'? For I remember that, pondering on Hengel's book *The Son of God*, I saw that the Trinitarian godhead is not first known by speculation about the Logos but comes out of the very Jewish idea of the son, Jesus as the Jewish Son of God par excellence.

Still, what death did for Jesus, just because it lets him be as the co-equal Son, must not be understood as exceptional in a way that stops us seeing its modelling, exemplary character. What shows him to be God incarnate shows us to be 'Sons in the Son'. And isn't it odd that phrases like that became clichés to be heard with a yawn, whereas actually the phrase names the very grounding of that knowable-to-us character of the dead that we call the Communion of Saints.

To believe in Jesus, 'Son of God in power with the resurrection from the dead in the sanctifying Spirit' (Romans 1:4) is to believe that our dead are now their real selves as they could not be in life. It is to believe that some of our dead have been so outstandingly ego-free in life that they are to be honoured and prayed to 'in heaven'.

There is a foundation, in contemplative thinking, for seeing the dead in a condition that is advantageous over us and thus prayable to, and 'for' of course! For we haven't a clue as to the way they are, except that they are their true selves as opposed to the selves-in-hiding that we all are now.

In sum: as Jesus, now raised, is all of himself as the Son of the Most High, so our dead are, or rather are becoming, all of themselves in him.

'Or rather ...' Surely the value of the doctrine of Purgatory is that it injects a healthy realism into a vague funeral parlour optimism. Because of who Jesus was, death brought him straight into the luminous reality of his Godhead. It will bring out the true self in us, but gradually.

The vision of the dead in a process of transformation, revealed to St Catherine of Genoa and immortalised by Dante in the *Purgatorio*, is exactly what is implied if we consider that death, which is immediately transformative in the case of Jesus as the universal pioneer self-giving victim, is transformative for all who follow him not immediately but by degrees. One of those jabs of nostalgia that conclude the *Waste Land* of Eliot is *poi s'ascose nel foco che gli affina*, 'then he leapt back into the fire that refines them' from the *Purgatorio* (XXVI.148). 'Eternal fire' would be the lot of those who forever refuse to die.

Now is the time to think of the dead, achieved and still in purgation. Only now we are able to do so with a much better paradigm: Jesus, the pioneer of our faith, died for us and thus came immediately into the risen state where he is all that he is and could not yet be while on earth. Those who follow him, they too, become all that they are and could not be on earth, all bound up with ego and its claims, so that they are being reconciled to being dead in degrees of purgation.

4.3 The Empty Tomb

Christ is dead and buried – facing this also means facing our own death, a preview of our own annihilation. Without recognising the violent reality of Christ's murder, we cannot comprehend the loving reality of his resurrection.

Death does two things for us. It threatens us with extinction and it rids us of those who threaten us. It frightens and it palliates. When Jesus, finally, was executed, this was awful of course, but also it meant the end of the disturbed life he'd got them into. Then the women found the tomb empty, the body gone. This had a shattering effect, and Rowan Williams says that we can still trace its terror in our texts.

For what happens when death fails to dispose of the disturber? It means that the *other* power of death comes upon them with full force: death as extinction. They are thrown into it. And it is into those thus thrown into a no-man's-land that he shows himself. Exposed to *their* death, they meet *him* alive. I cannot stop thinking about this, for it is the dangerous memory that keeps the church in being, of people who have died with him into a life without death. The whole Easter rhetoric arises out of this. It has, I think, been my life's task to get behind this rhetoric, to show how we die and live for ever.

The point is the effect of the empty tomb on them, on the women first. To begin with, this effect has no parallel in experience. It is like nothing on earth. If it isn't a case of grave-robbery, it's outlandish. But I am trying to say something more. The idea I am trying is that death is an experience that has two meanings. It means the end, our annihilation, what we know as 'me' come to a full stop. 'When you're dead you're dead' as theologians are saying to someone who is insisting that we have this immortal soul. 'I've still got a soul! That doesn't die!' Theologians point out that this sort of thinking is in denial of the real sense of our mortality. So that's the first meaning of death.

And the second is that death disposes of our victim. It gets rid of the tiresome Roberto Calvi whom people in the Vatican wanted dead. That's the second, the 'comfort' meaning. Now what I am arguing is that the discovery of the empty tomb *deprives* us of this meaning. And *then* I take the *logical* step, of saying that, deprived of the comforting meaning of death, the business-as-usual meaning, all that those people, the women and the rest, *have left* is the first, stark, annihilative meaning of death. I call this a logical step, algebraic if you like: death-as-extinction minus death as 'back to life as normal' which is death as ego-reassurance, equals death as extinction in all its starkness, blankness.

But this is still only a logical, a quasi-algebraic step: death-as-annihilation minus death as 'return to normal ego-life' equals death, our death, my death in all its starkness as if for the first time. Notice how I add words to enhance the rhetoric here. I am asking the reader: is it really, experientially, not just logically, the case that, deprived of the comfort of 'well he's dead and it's all over, back to life as we've always known it and endured it', being deprived of this palliative brings *their* death on them with the force of a tidal wave? This is what I am suggesting. In my favour is the fact that the finding of the tomb empty isn't like anything else, it's an experience never had before, at least as other than the obvious meaning of grave-robbery. As the experience has no category, I am saying what I like about it. But seriously, am I pointing to a unique, imaginable encounter by them of death as it really is, of their own death, a kind of preview of annihilation? I rather like that one, a preview of total annihilation …

If there *was* this, then the coming-to-them of Jesus, himself as never before, gets right into them, and 'annihilates annihilation'! This is important. If the paradigm of Christian faith-experience of life-after-death, or life more than death, is *that*, we have something validly reassuring for a Catholic brought up on the immortality of the soul, something a lot better than 'when you're dead you're dead,' leaving it at that. We are able to *mean* 'when you're dead you're dead' in a way that comes into contact with the risen presence.

4.4 A Nuclear Explosion

The faith which the empty tomb demands is not easy – it is not an intellectually held opinion but a shattering inner change of heart, being stretched by truth into new life beyond the limits of the ego. The new reality of the risen Christ is the 'nuclear' explosion of a new consciousness.

I am trying to work out the implications of a possible discovery, made by Hurtado and Hengel, about the origins of Christian faith, namely the evidence, in the earliest formulations of faith, of a quasi-nuclear explosion in consciousness that found not contradictory but wonderfully cohering the adoration of Jesus and the monotheism of the community to which he was revealed, a cohering that found the Holy Spirit not as the *reconciling* of the divine man with the one only God but as the sheer abundance of the Son–Father relationship in a new theophany.

What are the implications of this? The main implication, which rather is the substance of the original experience, is that Christian faith is grounded on an original stretching of the mind, a 'change of heart' that has intellectual as much as moral and practical dimensions, a being stretched beyond everything that can be thought of as intellectual conviction, that 'God has made both Lord and Christ this Jesus whom you crucified', as Peter said to the people at the beginning of Acts (2:36). The disciple who has 'seen the Lord' is, in that act, beyond himself or herself.

Now this original stretching of the mind by the heart felt to have burned within, as the Emmaus story tells us, means that faith is significantly more than finding the Jesus story, with the church's claims for it, convincing. Someone was saying to me only the other day that the distinction between finding the story convincing and deciding that I believe is so lost on people that Christians find themselves trying to convince people – if they are even doing this – as though this is what faith is all about. That further, decisive step for myself is lost, so that becoming a Christian is a matter of being convinced, and not a matter of undergoing the most important of changes, which is joining a community of believers not because they agree with me but because I am drawn to what holds them together – which involves, among other things, a totally changed attitude to death. Death cannot be final for one who believes that Christ is risen.

And it's more complicated than this, and not to the advantage of the would-be evangelist. For what is happening is that the groundedness of faith in a certitude beyond conviction has survived as a dogmative position with no accompanying aid to undergoing the stretching beyond the ego that is what underlies this dogmatic affirmation. So Christian belief in Jesus as Son of God 'in the sanctifying Spirit' (Romans 1:1) comes to be seen as 'what these Christians believe about a memorable first-century Jewish rabbi'. For, come to think of it, the disappearance, from the whole discussion, of that shattering inner change of heart, which supports Christian belief, reduces what Christians believe about Jesus to an opinion, to their opinion. 'No, I've been seized by what I believe; it brings *me* together in a way I don't really understand.' Who has entered with all of himself – or herself – into the mind of Paul when he says 'my trust is in the Son of God who loved me and gave himself for me'? No of course, we aren't all Paul, but can you see the shape of what I am saying, the seizing and changing of the heart to issue in a decision that, undramatically in most cases, underlies the act of faith?

This change of heart, which the Buddha says is the greatest of all miracles, is the heart of Christian belief, and if we are to speak of it in comprehensible psychological terms, as surely we must, we must speak of it as being stretched by truth beyond the ego.

I find myself asking what is so particularly distasteful to intelligent people today in what C. S. Lewis called 'same old Christianity'? And here I begin to contradict myself. For I want to say, on the one hand, that people are bored because Christian preaching does not stretch one beyond the ego, and on the other hand that people dislike Christianity because it *is* stretching, indeed dismantling the ego in which our culture is making us believe to an extent that is morbid.

And *am* I contradicting myself here? The discontent of an ego-centred culture with the challenge to the ego that I believe to be grounded in a transcendent revelation, the first Jesus moment, is a proper sense of *being failed by* the church/churches, which registers at a shallower level as 'the church is a bore'.

It has suddenly occurred to me that to preach the gospel without giving hints of the mental exercise that is essential to receiving it is like selling a complicated piece of hardware without a user's manual. What is so tantalising is that the main dogmatic formula, of the triune God, originally came at white heat *as* the stretching of minds into the God-head active in Jesus through the Spirit.

To come into this changes a person. Otherwise, as 'what Christians believe', it becomes a bore. That essential stretch beyond the self happens when 'This is convincing' becomes 'I believe'. This experience, or this kind of experience, is surely the pre-evangelising that people need today.

Here is what Karl Jaspers had to say about this a long time ago.

> Because religion is of such prime importance, awareness of my deficiency made me eager to hear what was being said in religious circles. It is among the sorrows of my life, spent in the search for truth, that discussion with theologians always dries up at crucial points; they fall silent, state an incomprehensible proposition, speak of something else, make some categoric statement, engage in amiable talk, without really taking cognizance of what one has said – and in the last analysis they are not really interested. For on the one hand they are certain of their truth, terrifyingly certain; and on the other hand they do not regard it as worth while to bother about people like us, who strike them as merely stubborn. And communication requires listening and real answers, forbids silence or the evasion of questions; it demands above all that all statement of faith (which are after all made in human language and directed towards objects, and which constitute an attempt to get one's bearing in the world) should continue to be questioned and tested, not only outwardly but inwardly as well. No one who is in definitive possession of the truth

can speak properly with someone else – he breaks off authentic communication in favour of the belief he holds.[2]

4.5 How Can We Stop Forgetting We Are Loved?

On Saturday night, the scapegoat-victim laid in the tomb rises again – this is deeply disturbing. All that we wanted to dispose of comes back to love us.

> Was it a terrifying act of love
> That led him into everybody's hell
> And answered only to the one above
> Whose certainty incomprehensible
>
> Made him complicit with his torturers
> On his own pioneering suicide
> The void befriended, body made a curse
> So that by his own will for us he died
>
> To show as that our victim is divine
> Thus overturned our murder-ordered world
> His resurrection an astounding sign
> To a humanity still foetal-curled.
>
> In a new terror, all our landmarks moved
> How can we stop forgetting we are loved?

We are used to thinking, if at all, of the burial of Jesus only as a physical event. But it was not so for those involved, whether disciples, friends or enemies. It was for everyone involved a psychological event, the disposal of the scapegoat-victim. It was an event in the consciousness of his disciples. It cannot be dissociated at all from what we do with things that trouble us. The psyche is a spontaneous undertaker.

So think in a new way of the burial of Jesus as what we all do with things that trouble us and that we would be rid of. Jesus after all is the conscience of humanity, and we bury him as we pursue our busy way, wanting all that troubles us to go away. A woman recently made the subtle comment that perhaps doubting Thomas, part of him, *wanted* Jesus dead, and this part put up a resistance to the news that he was alive again. When he *did* see Jesus, he was overcome and gave us the first high Christology: 'my Lord and my God'.

The women discovered the tomb empty, and this was a source of consternation In an early book on the resurrection, Rowan Williams said that we find echoes of this shock and bewilderment in our accounts of the Easter event.

The *source* of this consternation is this: our scapegoat victim has refused to be disposed of! The whole order of our psyche is upset, if we will pay a new kind of attention to ourselves that the Gospel now requires of us. As Girard says, we often don't know who our scapegoats are. But they're all in the body they buried.

If death has failed to dispose of our scapegoat-victim, then death has lost its power over us. For ever. The church conserves this dangerous memory, of death proved powerless and of us exposed to the draught of truth in a fearful world that we are to change. The church is God with us, and, *pace* a recent Roman statement, we can say where it is and we cannot say where it is not.

Hear the real church telling us that our scapegoat, undisposed of, is risen to embrace us in love, to which we breathlessly respond with faith, hope and charity.

5

Sunday Morning – Transformed Body

Christ's risen body is transformed; his followers, the women first, meet him, and recognise him beyond the empty tomb. This changes their reality forever; the only response is to live in a completely new way, and we need new language to describe it.
(Lakoff's New Enlightenment[1])

New Life in the living body dawns on Sunday morning – Christ's risen body is transformed, as ours will be. When the women and then the men saw that Christ had risen, they felt it in their bodies. Their hearts burned within them; this fire of love is a powerful transformative force.

The risen body of Christ is beyond death and life as we know it – it is a new kind of body. Sunday morning shatters the boundary between life and death, destabilising all categories of desire and vindication as we understand them.

So the resurrection means a new, embodied way of understanding. We know Christ is risen not by the light of reason, but because it's a true story. The meaning of the story is a life lived lovingly, and it is told in a new kind of language.

The dawn light of Sunday morning gives us new bodies and a new story – it is unstoppable. The transformed body of the risen Christ transforms our way of living.

5.1 Hearts on Fire

When the women and the men saw that Christ had risen, they felt the joy of it in their bodies. Their hearts burned within them; this fire of love is a transformative force, overcoming the powers of this world.

The women's shattering discovery
Resonates in the heart as in the head
The one definitive finality
Knows a disturbance, ending of the dead

Reversed in consciousness to consternation
Of women with a fear new on the earth
Which registered the depth of incarnation
Hinted an all unprecedented birth.

Then heart heard the most radical 'fear not!'
Of all the instances of the good news
Of him the first-born of the dead begot
Salvation that most deeply we may choose.

And when they saw him, never was such joy
In all the earth, this one without alloy.

The first Christian hymn perhaps: Philippians 2:6–11

Whence do we have this most ancient Christian hymn, already quoted in an early letter, sung by a Jewish sect, that equates its leader with the All-Highest of that severe monotheism, describes him degraded as only their imperial colonisers knew how to degrade, acquiring thence the name that is above names, the sacred Tetragrammaton of Judaism?

Whence do we have this outlandish cry of praise, celebrating its hero in the depths of his degradation by a hated imperial coloniser and now said to be reigning as the All-Holy reigns, his praise in defiance alike of his people's colonisers and forgetful of its own proud contempt for their gods in claiming divinity for a man?

Whence do we have this hymn of praise, in the circumstances of this one, if not from some explosion of consciousness at seeing him as he is, raised from the dead, a seeing which this sect claims to have had and been born of?

Such an explosion of consciousness has been detected by two noted New Testament scholars, Martin Hengel and Larry W. Hurtado, both of whom use language suggestive of an earthquake.

What was it like to see him again after 'l'horreur humaine de la crucifixion'? After he had been disposed of by the Roman method? It had all been a dream, this movement he had them in, his dream, as they returned to normal, the huge oppressive normal that the power of Rome could easily restore.

When they saw him, was it as though it hadn't happened, a typical dream of the bereaved? Not if we pay attention to the way they recalled to each other, 'did not our hearts burn within us while he walked with us and told us why he *had* to go through all that to fulfil the scriptures?' The awakening of the heart to be on fire with love was tied to the fittingness of an event that on the face of it was the triumph of the heart's numbness in face of the reality of the only power we know. Seeing him again, the way it seems to have happened and been remembered, had the terrible implication that world power was finished for them, that what they now were was the challenge to world power by the almighty power of love that vindicated this victim beyond the vindictiveness that keeps us under the system. To be *thus* empowered in face of the power of this world must have been, at least, unnerving! This dangerous joyousness shows itself in the *Acts* of the first martyrs.

What would happen to it when Rome adopted the church as its official religion? Surely the birth of monasticism is the answer to this question. Once awakened to a power over power as everyone knows it, the soul could not go to sleep again. Monasticism was a continuation of martyrdom by other means: as a rather lugubrious brother once put it, monastic life is martyrdom by instalments. The people who went into the desert were continuing the overcoming of the world achieved by Jesus and promised to those who follow him. Do we ever feel like people for whom the world has shot its bolt?

5.2 Risen Body

The risen body of Christ is not a corpse returned to life like Lazarus, but a transformed body which defies categorisation, breaking down the divide between dead and living. Christ's transformed body breathes new life into our bodies too.

N. T. Wright says something vital about the resurrection.[2] The disciples were not just documenting a miraculous event, Jesus come to life out of the tomb. They were doing this of course, but only as implied in what they were really impelled to do, which was to say that Jesus is now alive as never before, and we have to catch up with him in his new life, life beyond life, that we're now in, just, breathlessly. This life was his now, and they and we were in it, caught up in it. Hence Rowan Williams' statement that if they were documenting the miraculous coming to life of a dead body they were making a remarkably bad job of it. They weren't. They were catching up, breathlessly as it were, with where he was now, calling them.

What was discovered makes an enormous demand on reason, which might be avoided by saying there was a mistake – they got the wrong tomb. Now here comes the tricky bit. If that unaccountable movement of the mind and heart that is supernatural faith responds to the empty tomb as integral to the shock of God's invasion, we must be very careful not to impose on the mind thus shaken the needless further burden of imagining a dead body coming to life and 'emerging' (N. T. Wright's word) from the tomb. Forget the raising of Lazarus – or rather remember it as a deliberate example of what the Resurrection was not. This restraint is reinforced by the statement of Aquinas – who wouldn't have shared our distrust of the miraculous – that the resurrection was not only unwitnessed but unwitnessable. The most that we can say is that somehow, at a given moment, the body was no longer there. Wright's insistence that the faithful person imagine the emergence of the body from the tomb is the one mistake in his marvellous account, a mistake that is strange in the light of his own uniquely insightful observation that the risen body of Jesus is somehow – and what a 'somehow'! – in two worlds, ours and that of the unknown one: for it is odd if this elusively dual existence *began* in our world alone, as the emergence of a body from a tomb.

When I was teaching in Marquette University in the States, the question being asked was: if a TV camera had been placed appropriately, would it have picked up anything? I am sure that Aquinas would have been intrigued by the question, and answered: 'suddenly, presumably, there was nothing there', and would have hastily added, 'and that was not the Resurrection, but an odd and unavoidable fall-out, what scientists call, when they don't know what else to say, a singularity.'

The main difficulty is that we are accustomed to think of the resurrection as something that happened to Jesus, an amazing isolated prodigy, a dead man come to life – this on the one hand, on the other hand we are called to a new life 'like he has now'. But *how* was the new life 'like' his, seen as a new kind of existence, that of a glorified body 'whatever that may be?' This was my problem at the very beginning of attempting to understand, as a novice. I felt it at an Easter Mass, done by Abbot Trafford when I was still a novice, which seemed to be celebrating a miracle *and* a new life for all of us, a new consciousness. But the sheer miracle seemed to stop at itself. It didn't immediately suggest a new life for us. The new life was 'like' the miraculous event, but that word 'like' didn't say how. Our new life, which was spiritual, was 'like' a 'glorified body, 'whatever that is'. On the one hand a cosmological puzzle. On the other, our life totally transformed. How does the first draw us into the second? It doesn't, unless it is, for us, for the disciples, him as he is now saying come on, join me who have called the bluff of death and am now the wisdom of God where all the impossible things I said about being as the birds of the air etc. and my Father taking care of you come true. *This* was what it was like to feel 'saved', pulled into the life of Jesus and trying to catch up. But when the resurrection ceases to mean that, we think of it as a prodigious miracle, coming to life of a dead body, an amazing isolated event. The resurrection becomes the icing on the cake of a mysterious 'salvation', which theologians start thinking of in a quite different way, all to do with 'vicarious satisfaction' on the part of a God-Man, the Anselmian idea, Jesus making up for the 'infinite offence' of Adam's sin, something Jesus fixed with God, not something we are drawn into, Jesus-alive. So we have the astonishing fact that this new life that the disciples were trying to catch up on, the saved life, the trans-formed life, the life beyond life as we know it, life after death *in this life*, salvation in substance, the thing itself, was not mentioned when theolo-gians explained how Jesus saves us! The resurrection became the icing on the cake.

This is the root of the division of Jesus, into the dogmatic Jesus who 'really rose' and the Sermon-on-the-Mount Jesus who challenges us to *dare* as the resurrection *enables* us to. My mind's attempt to get together the prodigious event and life changed for ever – the prodigy of Jesus risen, and him as a new way to live, pervaded the Easter liturgy for me. I don't know about you, but perhaps you recognise my problem. Jesus risen as our pioneer pulling us into his new way of living and thinking has been nearly forgotten. We are left with two things: an isolated prodigious event, and a call to fuller life somehow modelled on Jesus risen.

When we get into his new stride, it is as though we had died already and so are not to be terrorised. By Baptism we *have* died already – that is difficult to take in, but becomes very real as it was for them. The Easter faith shares in the daring of our pioneer and so is prepared for whatever is to come with global warming and the like. Above all, it is a new consciousness such as Eckhart Tolle gives a taste of. It is not only its taste but its sacrament and substance.

The living and the dead

To have seen, to have had manifest to me, the risen Jesus, is to model on him and thus, as he has, to have died. But to live in this world as one who has died is to be estranged from a mental world of 'the living and the dead'. In thus dividing us into 'the living and the dead', death exercises over us a *'divide et impera!'*: 'divide and so rule'; it rules us by dividing us into these two batches or herds of humanity.

Further, we seal this pact with death by the device of sacrificing a human victim. This is found to pacify the tribe, but the peace thus made is a peace with dividing and ruling death.

Where is Jesus dead to be placed in this drama, he the sacrificed for political peace à la Caiaphas, and, on the full theological scale, sacrificed as our universal victim? We have to take a step further and say that this victim, far from appeasing the God of our invention who needs appeasing, reveals through his risenness the real God who is only love and knows nothing of our sordid deals with death.

Now what happens to Jesus as one among the dead *in so far as* we are limiting ourselves to this world ruled by death? He ceases to be 'one among the dead' the moment we let in the vision of him risen and thus are no longer mentally in the world ruled and divided by death. But his corpse is the visible and immemorial sign that he *is* among the dead. So, since he is not and cannot be among the dead, this sign is absent.

And this is how it worked for the disciples: they were drawn into the vision of him risen and so were able to see the empty tomb *not*, as the commonsense faithless mind will see it, as the start of a whodunnit, but as the blazing sign that he is not among the dead. And this is exactly what the women hear from the angel: 'Why are you looking for the living among the dead?' This is not just a 'poetic' way of saying 'why are you looking for someone alive as though he were dead?' It is evoking the whole lived anthropology of bereavement and mourning, the whole language of 'the living and the dead'. Normally, the living are in one mental place, the dead in another, but here, in the empty tomb, these categories are abolished: the newly and divinely living has no place among the dead. The violent dying and rising of Jesus possesses the mind and heart, so that those we *call* the dead are no longer in that category but now, as Anthony Kelly brilliantly argues, 'populate the world of realised eschatology initiated by the rising of Jesus'.[3] Our dead, our Christian dead, our dead in Christ the revealed mercy of God, are *not* 'among the dead'. So that Paul can say that in the end we who are alive will 'by no means' be ahead of those who are dead. In the new age, the dead are not left behind us in our march to nowhere, they're waiting for us where they are in him.

The corpse is made to be absent from the tomb to remove the immemorial sign that he who has died is among the dead. He is *known* to be not among the dead by the heart that burns and not, apart from this vision and transformation, by his absence from the tomb.

Mere absence from the tomb does not say that he is not among the dead. It merely says that presumably he's somewhere else. We cannot overstate the depth to which the vision of the risen one goes down to the marrow of us with its destabilising power, abolishing our categories of 'the living and the dead'. For the live believing disciple, these categories are obsolete.

C. H. Dodd, the great biblical scholar, had the interesting idea that the New Testament writers felt the empty tomb as a fact but an encumbrance – which makes them the more credible; they had no inclination to invent it. They had to mention it because it was there, a funny kind of a stray fact, not because it made more manifest the not-among-the-dead character of Jesus and his followers. This is a kind of proof of the truth of the empty tomb: they had no need to invent it. I think that a more mature vision does need to invent it, to invent it in synch with its revealed facticity, to be able to relish the words of the angel, 'why seek the living among the dead?' The empty tomb as fact had to be grown up to spiritually, perhaps.

I am deeply moved by this image of death as a tyrant, made tyrannical by our addiction to our life, grimly dividing us up into two batches like the commandant of a death camp. The death camp is a colony of death as king, mimetically celebrating the manner of his rule, dividing us up into batches. It all helps me to take deeply into myself the freedom with which Christ has made us free, not any old freedom but the kind he gives, to which the soft spot in me glows with the memory of long-standing prayer.

Christian hope penetrates into the world of hopeless grief. Death is not a grim barrier separating the living from those who have passed from the world before us. The resurrection disrupts the power of death, and the meaning of time itself. As the risen Christ is the anticipation of the future, those who are with him are no longer lost in the past, but already populate the eschatological future in store for all. Despite the obscurity of the apocalyptic rhetoric, the message is clear: '... We who are alive ... will by no means precede those who have died' (Galatians

4:15), but will be caught up into a new order of existence with them, to meet Christ in his final appearance, 'so that we will be with the Lord forever'.[4]

Common sense says the dead are in the past, they are behind, we forging ahead – to nowhere! But faith says they are in Christ our future, they are not lost in the past but already populate the eschatological future in store for all. So 'we who are alive will by no means precede those who have died.' Why 'by no means', why this emphasis? It is to counteract the common-sense notion that they, being dead, are 'behind', we who are alive are 'before'. This book puts an electric current right through the New Testament from beginning to end.

5.3 Desire Destabilised

The resurrection effect – the transformation of Sunday morning – leaves us with a challenge to live in the world it has opened up. It shatters all categories, destabilises our desires and replaces vindictive justice with vindication in love.

'The Resurrection' meant, both at once, an event, Jesus-encounters and his tomb empty, and a new world now lived in, for people to be admitted to by complex rituals, centred on the baptism, naked, and reclothed. The difference between Baptism and Eucharist was vital, for it was the difference between a state come out of darkness and being and living in and enjoying the light. What Kelly calls the 'Resurrection Effect' is the luminous combination, nearly impossible to recover, of event and transformative celebration, a celebration obsessed with the difference between the world left – of sin and sadness – and the world now lived in, and the difference that *this* entailed between the coming-into of Baptism and the being-in of Eucharist. The latter difference vibrates with the same energy as the difference between the world left behind and the world entered. The whole thing, as we learn to make it articulate in its parts, has a coherence like the astonishing coherence of a hologram. What is closed off to us, without a combination of faith and active imagination, is the mind that underwent that passage from darkness to light. Closed to us, above all, is what made the whole thing so desperately and absolutely *matter* to the men and women concerned. Of course this was 'the Resurrection'. But what we only begin to get a glimpse of is how so much came of so limited-to-an-event. Not, be it noted, so much of so little, but so general of so specific, so universal out of so local.

Of course what makes it so difficult for us to grasp this combination of the specific and the universalised is the biggest difference-in-sameness of all, that between the Jesus who was killed and buried and the mysterious man of heaven sporadically encountered. At times it seems to me that the sameness between the man of horror and the man of glory must have been the most blindingly luminous of all.

For all this to come together requires a destabilising of desires of exceptional intensity. The seeker is confronted with so many details that, as they stand, provoke the intellectual impatience that has been – I now see for the first time! – my besetting fault. The gentle injunction to 'let all this come together' I become conscious of as I read a recent article that sets out all the detail of the earliest baptismal catechesis, and a murmured, 'take it in, and wait, and let light come!' Slowly I discern what those people, in an age so remote from ours, were excited about and concerned to imprint on their new candidates.

Once the Resurrection has happened or, better, begun, the problem is how to live in the world that it has opened. But what have I been exploring in these last days but the destabilising of egoic desire, of the way the ego has us looking at the world. For the normal ego-organised consciousness, what I see around me are people and things happening to which I must react and do so as these appear attractive or to be avoided. Especially things pertaining to my job, my position in society with its opportunities and hopes and fears. How does the fact of Jesus risen and touching me impinge on this whole system? It will destabilise my outlook. I cannot find a better word than destabilise for the total changing of my attitude to life. And I cannot think of a better word than this same destabilising to describe what the Spirit does for the disciples caught up in the Resurrection effect. *Without* this concept in all its psychological radicality, the words I might come up with for what the Spirit does are words like 'comfort', 'console for the loss of Jesus' – the miserable basis of faith envisaged by a dear friend of mine – all words in what we might call the moral order, the order of good advice among friends. But what is involved for people baptised in the dead-and-risen one is not to be conveyed by any such conventional, grief-addressed words.

Not surprisingly, John the Seer has three very unobvious words for what the Spirit will do for them. They are descriptions of how the world will look to the awakened disciple. This world will find itself exposed by the Spirit as, first, in sin ('because they haven't believed in me'), of righteousness ('because I go to the Father'). What is the reasoning here?

Ronald Knox is baffled by it and makes of the going to the Father the
introduction of a new topic: 'it is to the Father I am going – by the way' –
but John's reasoning here is that Jesus' going to the Father *vindicates* him
against the world, his righteousness versus theirs – the logic *is* logical –
and 'judgement because the world is already judged' by the vindication
of Jesus: the righteousness of the new situation has gone into judicial
effect.

The curious logic of John has the Resurrection effect wind its way
round in the already distorted desire-system of the world. This is John's
primitive version of what I am calling the destabilising of desire, the
exposure of desire as 'mine' in a heavily ironic sense.

> Desire destabilised lets beauty in,
> Bypassed the censor whose intolerance
> Keeps us respectable in mortal sin
> And unacquainted with the inner dance.

> This tolerance lets in the infinite
> And makes religion possible and fun
> For theologians to adore and fit
> Together some things new under the sun.

> But when the theologians conform
> They make theology a thought-police
> Will not protect the faithful from the storm
> Of clever minds the enemies of peace,

> But always the last word is with desire
> Of the original creating fire.

Vindication with love

> Vindication with no vindictiveness
> Is beautiful, but it cannot be known
> The body still there to embalm and bless
> And show the murderer who must atone

> The new robs death of power to keep the dead
> Visible to accuse and keep unlove
> The norm: but now the breaking of the bread
> Him vanished for the heart at last to move

And know the world a stranger minus death
With love the only order in its place
For prayer to taste upon a steady breath
That is the body's metaphor of grace

That's not dependent on tired rhetoric
Knows death dissolved, with life no longer sick.

The dead keep our vindictiveness alive
So Jesus unvindictive vindicated
Nullifies death just where it has to thrive:
His is a consummation long awaited

Where death is undone, not in rhetoric
But in emotional reality
Shows what we call reality as sick:
Jesus I love you showing this to me

In a connection that must now amaze
Of deathlessness with non-vindictiveness
That robs death of its power to void our praise
Of substance, our eternity of yes

Whose grammar is the oldest bond we know,
This meal your flesh and blood on which to grow.

The truth that pierces me this Easter and that I'm trying to express in these sonnets is that Jesus risen represents that wholly new and unprecedented thing, vindication with love – the burning heart on the way to Emmaus – in place of vindictive justice. This absence of vindictiveness from vindication sears the soul and takes the terror out of death, I'm not quite sure how, but I know it does and try to put this conviction into this piece of didactic verse.

Two good words: 'The priority of joy is a minority report filed by Christians and children.' And: 'Jesus is the song of the world' (a boy of twelve in catechism class).

5.4 New Enlightenment

How can we know Christ is risen? Not because it is a fact verifiable by reason,
but because it's a true story with a meaning. The meaning is a life lived lovingly,
in community. To express the meaning of this story we need a new language.

A new age

The body hugs itself in love with you
Creator, wired in it your reason's word[5]
In worship of the absolutely true
To refuse which inclines to be absurd.

Your reason in us is our drama too
Entails the crucifixion of the Word
Who draws the few awakened to the new
In to their deepest regions being stirred

Whom resurrection woke to more than life
Along with the command to spread the news
Of the high way other than ceaseless strife
That in the depths of me have still to choose.

O may I then be poised to be set free
Resisting nothing that will threaten me!

Grappling with the New Enlightenment

Take the statement: 'Jesus saves us from the power of death.' It is
generally assumed that this statement is understood, up to a point, 'by
the light of reason'. 'The power of death' is metaphorical, the metaphor
being the image of death as a tyrant who exercises power over our
minds instilling fear. But 'the light of reason' is a fiction, espoused by
Descartes and the Enlightenment, according to which reason gives us a
plain statement to the effect that Jesus affects us, while the metaphor is
an agreed departure from plain statement to add warmth. To the image
of a wily tyrant the mind responds with fear, and this fear Jesus
removes.

But what happens to this account when the light of reason, with its
cognate plain statements, is seen to be a fiction? Then the metaphor is no
longer an assistance to the light of reason, but pertains to the substance

of what is communicated by the statement that Jesus saves us from the power of death. For reason is nearly totally unconscious, and our only access to it is through metaphor and narrative, above all narrative. So what happens when I respond to the statement is that I receive its communication by allowing reason in me to become conscious in the narrative 'Jesus saves me'. So instead of saying that the statement employs a metaphor that I can respond to emotionally, I have to say that the statement gives to unconscious reason the narrative whereby it becomes conscious. Instead of saying that the statement is made and emotion is stimulated, I have to say that in the statement, reason is 'narrated' or 'narrified'. The huge revision is from metaphor as ornament to metaphor as substance.

I find that with this precision, the statement becomes more communicative of mystery. The moment when Lakoff really 'took' for me was when I realised that the notion that ordinary communication is 'literal' and metaphor ornamental is false. *All* rational communication is, in the broadest sense, metaphorical, storytelling.

This has implications, I suddenly see, for the statement of Christian belief. Take the belief, Jesus is risen from the dead. I will not say 'it is true for me that Jesus rose from the dead.' My colleague Mike McNulty SJ used to say to his philosophy class at the beginning of the year, 'I forbid you to say, so-and-so is true for me.' *You* may say this is true for *me*. I cannot. But what is entailed by this refusal in the light of Lakoff's disclosure that our only way for reason in me to express itself is by metaphor? If this is true, then I have to re-examine the notion that, for me, Jesus really did rise from the dead. For this 'really did' is not a fact stateable independently of my being asked to state it. Realism, for the believer, does not entail a factual status for 'Jesus rose' knowable apart from the metaphorical expression required for the fact to be stated at all. What Lakoff is doing is vastly to extend our dependence on mind-process by pointing out that the things self-evident to Enlightenment reason *are* self-evident *only* in and to the storytelling whereby reason comes into its own.

A further precision is called for in the matter of the Resurrection. What seems to have overwhelmed the disciples of Jesus was the realisation that the man they had seen, the 'heavenly man', the man in another reality beyond our common reality, was identically the man they had buried. It would seem that 'Jesus has risen' is the simple statement of this identity. But the meaning of the statement 'he is risen' is massively metaphorical, for it affirms that he has anticipated the resurrection of the

dead believed (by Pharisees, not Sadducees) to be destined to happen at
the end of time. Now what I learn from Lakoff is that this massively
metaphorical nature of the statement is only an extension of the *already*
metaphorical nature of the statement that he has risen. For gone is the
area of simply direct and non-metaphorical truth with which metaphor
can be contrasted as embellishment.

But we are not there yet. What of the statement 'the dead do not rise'?
If they do, they stop being dead. Real death has not occurred. So what of
the statement 'Jesus has risen'? It was based not on the tomb being
empty, but on encounters with a Jesus who was more himself than he
had ever been, that occasioned a 'burning of the heart' (in the Emmaus
story), with the empty tomb showing the identity between the new man
and the man buried, a devastating identity, stretching the mind almost
to breaking point. The *fact* of the empty tomb could be verified by any
passer-by. The *meaning* of the empty tomb could not – it was known only
to those whom the risen Jesus had awoken from sleep. And by 'the
meaning' I do not mean any of the pious thoughts you might have
reflecting on it. I mean the only alternative to a surmise of grave-
robbery.

Now what if the Enlightenment reason that says that a dead body
does not come to life is replaced by a new enlightenment that welcomes
the resurrection as meaning life expanded beyond its known limits to
mean the human community united in freedom from death, with Jesus
as 'the firstborn of the dead'? What if the freedom we naturally seek *is*
sought because reason in us is wired to find its meaning that way? What
if the freedom that, achieved in this way, asks 'what am I to do now?' Is
there no answer? Yes there is, the answer is 'act lovingly', act for
community. For this inclination to community *is* the inclination *of* freedom as this comes upon us. And it comes upon us in respect of the risen
one encountered. The risen Jesus, encountered, is the church in embryo.

If reason desires the Resurrection, what becomes of an apologetic for
which reason is inherently emotionless and sceptical: if reason welcomes the Resurrection, where are we?

That reason is thus hopeful puts me in mind of something Elizabeth
Anscombe said that was universally acclaimed: that we need a concept
of human flourishing. Why was this so manifestly a beautiful statement? Because, in the light of Lakoff, it was an act of passionate rational-
ity.

New Enlightenment language

To be saved by Christ from the power of death is a shattering experience, of being sucked down into a vortex of energy and, resisting nothing, to be annihilated into life beyond life and death. Yet at the liturgy we hear this explosion in consciousness described in the bland language of the daily paper, and it leaves us cold as the paper does. How are we to feel, under these words, the throb of annihilation into life beyond life and death?

First, we must expect it, by knowing how words fail it. But then we have to know why. The words are assembled, the colloquial translation is composed, on the assumption that being rational consists in consulting the light of reason, thought to hover over us, strong in the intelligent, weak in the stupid. Wrong. Neuroscience has demonstrated that reason is not ours in this cool, unemotional way, but is almost entirely unconscious, so that our only expression of it is through a vast array of symbols, the 'forêts des symboles' of Baudelaire,[6] and above all, through *stories*. Hearing a generous story, hearing the life of a saint as Ignatius did while he was convalescing and was bored, the complex circuitries of our neurons, especially the recently discovered mirror-neurons, are fired, and we want to come together in a community that honours the sacred.

Now this mechanism was thrown into a paroxysm for those who followed Jesus to the bitter end where they were scattered, the annihilative force of the Spirit working in them. Then the Spirit that had dispersed them assembled them at the encounters with Jesus risen. The follow-through of this encounter was the devastating realisation that the newly mysterious man of heaven was identically the man they had followed, abandoned to a horrendous death, and buried.

We, hearing this story, could pick up the throb of the event under the words, even under their laconic compression into the formula: Jesus saves us from the power of death through the torment of the cross and consummating resurrection.

By all accounts, the new Vatican translations are a feeble attempt to recover the throb of the great story by artificially detrivialising the language with Latinate archaisms. The See of Peter should know better, for Peter carries the memory of denial, tears, and the confirming of his brethren. And this, all this, when science is into a New Enlightenment!

If reason in us welcomes resurrection,
Of reasoned faith we have to think again,

If thinking is allergic to dejection
This calls for reassessment of our pain.

The ancient saying 'too good to be true'
Calls for rethinking, for it may be based
On reason as detached from me and you,
And so our reason may be two-way faced:

An old addiction to unhappiness
Comes from our birth into a history
Of woes and war and long familiar stress
Of which no one of woman born is free.

And so bad news inherited is faced
With optimism that of God is graced.

5.5 The Nature of Light

The dawn light of Sunday morning gives us new bodies and a new story – it is unstoppable.

New consciousness, new anthropology
Implodes into the gospel to release
Light into reaches they can hardly see
Who know only the Bible and its peace.

The shock of resurrection sends its waves
Into a new world culture that would form
That would spell out how spirit now behaves
In an impatience with the Bible's norm.

The science built upon this norm alone
We call theology, and it looks old
To eyes now opened to what can be known
Of us in history now newly told.

And the heart become nothing in deep prayer
Welcomes new light that comes from everywhere.

'No one after lighting a lamp covers it with a vessel, or puts it under a bed, but puts it on a stand, that those who enter may see the light' (Luke 8:6–18), the gospel reading for today, on which the following is my homily.

Jesus uses, for the proclamation of the Good News, the image of light. Light is recognised by scientists as being on the border between science and mystery. By its instaneity, it defies all attempts to control it. And as Michael Ramsay, the great Archbishop of Canterbury, never ceased to point out, the composers of all our New Testament literature are saturated with the explosion of consciousness, spread by the Holy Spirit throughout the world, that occurred when it became known that the luminous presence that floored and blinded Saul of Tarsus who spent the rest of his life telling people about it, that this luminous presence was, identically, the man who had been brutally executed by the powers of this world, both religious and secular. I think I have only just been bowled over by this identity, and no one who hasn't felt it can understand the New Testament which is its fallout. When Jesus uses the ridiculous image of lighting a lamp and putting it inside a pot, he is saying, to all and sundry, 'You can't stop it!'

One ecclesial mentality has been trying to stop it ever since. One may suspect an attempt to stop it when the interpretation of the Second Vatican Council which is offered by Giuseppe Alberigo, the editor of the *History of Vatican II*, which is the standard work, rated with Jedin's *History of the Council of Trent* (4 volumes, 1951–76), is described as espousing 'a hermeneutic of rupture'.

Light broke out at Pope John's Council, and words are not going to stop it.

5.6 Living Body: The Beginning

The transformed body of the risen Christ transforms our way of living, in our bodies infused with Christ's new life.

Villanelle for the Risen One

I know you risen when I am in mind
Too wonderful our history today
But I remember 'seek and you will find'.

We do not recognise that we are blind
Until we find the way within to pray
And learn of you that you are all and kind.

We have not known till now the inner way
We think ahead but we are still behind
And live by night half-hopeful for the day.

We live content with nothing but the rind
And yet the fruit is there for our assay
All is available to humankind

Will not believe our luck and all we may
So we prefer eternally to wind
Around in night and miss the blinding ray

Which is the Resurrection underlined
By history to be its final say:
I know you risen when I am in mind
As Saul was not till he was undermined.

The real Easter Gospel

When Jesus said to Levi in the tax office, 'Follow me!' and Levi simply did, when he said it to Simon, and Simon simply did, and the same with James and John and the others, he awoke something in them that is the deepest thing in us, the desire for life in its fullness beyond all our slowly learned expectations of it. It was this thing that he had awoken in them that kept them together, going they knew not where, supported by stories he kept telling about what he called the Kingdom, whatever that was, but they just knew he had it. To their growing consternation, this led to confrontation with everything they had come to know as security, and finally to the disaster of his arrest and execution and their total demoralising, bringing out the worst in everyone of cowardice and shame and betrayal and denial.

Now what is going on in the stories of him coming to them after all this, connected with reports of his tomb being found empty, is that the original desire he woke in them and that had led to disaster was now coming into an amazing fulfilment with him now as he truly was and is. The Easter stories are not the careful documentation of a prodigious miracle. If they were, as Rowan Williams has said, they were making a very bad job of it. But they weren't, they were breathlessly trying to catch up with him as he now was, a new being-together in something that they had to spread, what they called the good news, a new being together of people, persecuted and compelled to spread itself. The contagion of Jesus had caught on in the world, never to leave it whatever the crises we have to face in these dark times.

This was not a happy ending. It was an exciting beginning, and it was all about him as he is now, we his body, living, each, not for himself but for him who is life itself. And all the horror had been necessary. The desire awakened by Jesus had to prove itself against the worst that the world could do. We, the church, have to reawaken it in this dark time. We must above all pray for the grace to do this.

6

Next Week – Beyond the Garden

Christ's followers are transformed too, their hearts are changed, which holds them together outside the resurrection garden. How can we share this new reality, becoming church in an inclusive, embodied way?

(James Alison's 'new catechesis'[1])

After the initial shock of the resurrection, it is time to leave the garden and get used to a changed life. This means living in the present, in readiness for whatever new life throws at us now – and it means embodied faith.

The good news of the risen body is a theology lived without fear of death or imperial power. The church, Christ's body, needs to overcome its own fear of losing power, so that all its members can hear each other speak.

Yet listening is not enough – the next step is to identify with each and every speaker. The way we live has had God for its victim, and so it has God for our saviour from it. If loving one's enemies is to become a reality, this means becoming a loving outsider, identifying with the enemy and befriending the victim, as Christ himself did.

The loving outsider draws all things into himself. The cosmic Christ of the new creation overcomes our exploitation of each other and of our earth. The gospel deprofessionalised is the simple fact that we are loved out of nothing into being and continually drawn together into a new creation. This gives us the confidence to follow the Spirit into a future which is not yet revealed ...

6.1 Out of the Garden: God for Now

The resurrection means readiness for whatever new life throws at us. The new consciousness of Christ's risen body takes a while for the disciples to absorb. The past life is not restored, but the future end is not upon them – it is time to live now.

Homily on Luke 12:35–38

The reading we have just heard speaks of readiness. Today we hear of nothing else, there's a list of cataclysms we have to be ready for – ecological collapse for humans, global monetary meltdown, some crucial eruption of violence into World War III. I'm sure there are others, but their names escape me.

Which one then? None of the above, which means all of the above. I mean the now. The conventional view about the early days of the church is, that *at first* they thought Jesus was to come again, 'any day now', and then, as he didn't, people settled down, saying 'O it's some sort of spiritual future, eschatology you know.' Thus the power of now was pushed out by the power of the banal, the conversation in the queue.

But it was the power of now which exploded in the consciousness of those who saw Jesus risen from the dead – even after he had 'vanished from their sight' they could say, 'did not our heart burn within us when he told us how he had to go through that horrible ordeal?' The risen Jesus is the power of now made visible only to disappear and leave the heart on fire, always able to be referred back to in our prayer. If we could catch that moment, in which, as he broke the bread, they saw who it was and he disappeared …

The power of now, revealed to a man on the point of taking his own life, is always drawing us – not back, but in. It has its own readiness.

> Disappear now into my unity
> Where there is only you for the whole world
> Ended the mental noise of me with me
> With love your banner over us unfurled.
>
> This pain is sharper than what I inflict
> On me in the attempt to satisfy
> According to the rules that I keep strict
> In order never to myself to die
>
> One with the victim of the sacrifice
> That the world makes to keep itself in place
> Carries me in the arms of loving thrice
> Into the grace beyond all our disgrace.
>
> This is the pain of a last ecstasy
> Of self from self torn ultimately free.

Jesus to love you do I dare the future,
Welcome it in me as whatever comes
And tease memory's ever-forming suture
Around the present with its comfort crumbs?

Is this the draught the soul has got to feel
Security unveiled idolatrous
Encouraging the spirit to congeal
With habit to deny me curious?

Mary who bore the future in her womb
Knew this high dare at the Annunciation,
The Son who would deny our comfort's tomb
To bring to birth man as God's incarnation.

I am the rower, as old Søren saw[2]
To love is to look round and to adore!

6.2 New Catechesis

How can the good news of the risen body of Christ shape a fresh and relevant theology, lived for now, recognising our own violence and vulnerability without sacralising the violence of the cross?

After a long phone conversation with James Alison, I begin to get a deeper and fuller idea about what he is, uniquely, engaged in. A new concept emerges, of a ministry currently non-existent in any recognisable form, yet very like what the teaching church seems to have been like in the patristic period before theology got specialised as a thing done by 'theologians', in the period when, as Anthony Bloom put it, theology came straight out of the experience of praying and worshipping. What James calls this is a 'catechesis', and I think it is something I have dreamed of: the church talking about itself as a way of making sense of life. Obviously, since we've had theology with its long history as a specialised attempt of faith to understand itself in the rough-and-tumble of the university, this new ministry *embraces* theology. In a way, it is an invitation to believers who want to understand *themselves* as believers. Alison's ministry is not just writing good theological books, of which he has half a dozen or so to his name. It is rather understanding

theology as the live consciousness of a Catholic Christian. It is addressing believers who have very understandably given up on having the
faith as the central light of their lives, light of a personal psychology.

But what *is* he doing, what is he about, other than 'writing stimulating
theology'? He himself gives us the clue. He is working on a new
catechesis, a new systematic instruction in the basics of faith. It is almost
as if we hadn't *had* the faith before he came along with his version of it.
It's only 'as if' of course. But what is it that suggests this exaggeration?
What is this new radicalism?

He is saying, in effect: 'Think your faith again. Think again your belief
in God and his Son Jesus crucified and risen and Spirit-giving.' Well, it's
always good to think again, not in the sense of 'having second thoughts'
but in the sense of freshening long-standing ones. But what is new in
this? Why is what he is about anything more than writing exciting
theology?

To answer this question, we must look to something on the face of it
extraordinary, namely the fact that the Christian faith itself has recently
acquired a new relevance to our life. There has been a quasi-seismic shift
in the ground of faith, that occasioned by the insights of René Girard.
This shift in the ground of Christian relevance is extraordinary. We have
discovered ourselves behaving in ways that, discernibly, crucify the Son
of God and call for divine forgiveness. The discovery of scapegoating as
our political stabiliser *secularises* the Passion of Christ and thus exposes
as escapist our *sacralising* of it. And so we have to learn anew the story of
Jesus as our own hitherto unacknowledged story, the story of the murder on which we build our fearful and cautious world.

Through the lens of Girard, we are to relearn our human story so that
it becomes a 'see-through' through which we see '*l'horreur humaine de la
crucifixion*' as Girard calls it. And this means that violence, the violence
we accept as a 'necessary evil', becomes an accepted sickness to which
God, in Jesus, is offering the cure.

So it is a matter of re-learning ourselves as violent yet vulnerable to
the grace of God, violence and vulnerability disturbingly alike.

In the pre-Girardian situation of catechesis, of the faith as taught, the
crucifixion is salvific because its victim has been tacitly sacralised as
'undergoing death for the salvation of the world'. The Constantine-
effect on the church can be understood as transforming the death of
Jesus by a lynch-mob with the support of worldly power, into 'a sacrifice', with the victim as the priest and the cross his altar. This of course
lets imperial power off the hook. The Christianised Emperor is not to see

himself and all he stands for as the murderer of Jesus, and it is entirely 'in character' that Constantine abolished crucifixion as a mode of punishment out of reverence for that august victim, who becomes, through this mental shift, sacralised on his cross. From being the most horrific, cruel and degrading of all punishments known, crucifixion becomes a unique privilege for him who 'reigns from the wood'.

Now in an important sense, this sacred victim, this victim made sacred by a piece of political self-evasion, has been the Christ of a pre-Girardian catechesis – it looks to us that way, we have to add, lest we make our present understanding absolute. This Christ 'saved us' by a sacrifice whose murderous character is ignored and which, *through* this evasion, is the basis of 'The Holy Sacrifice of the Mass'.

Tearing away the imperial veil of the sacrifice of the cross by the re-description of Calvary as murder, we are led to understand ourselves as murderers and open to a divine forgiveness that goes deeper into us than we can go into ourselves, and I recall a great Russian theologian as saying that faith is a self-knowledge we would not have by ourselves. Is this giving some idea of what Alison means by a new catechesis? The crucial insight goes like this: This is the post-Girardian question to ourselves – it demands a fresh paragraph.

How can we ever have thought that the *mystery* of our salvation consists in the *manner* in which it is accomplished, namely the Passion of Christ, the Sacred Passion? There's nothing mysterious in this, it's the way we run the world, man's inhumanity to man used as our political stabiliser. What is awesomely mysterious and *is* the mystery is that there is God, infinite, incomprehensible, absolute, who comes to us *through* our use of our stabiliser on him who, the deed once done, can reveal himself as the Son of God in power through the Spirit of sanctification (Romans 1:1), Jesus Christ yesterday, today, and the same for ever (Hebrews 13:8).

One of my first theological insights was that the task of theology is to say in what the mystery consists. Girard has been so radical as to say in what the mystery does *not* consist, and, even more radically, in where we have mistakenly placed it: the 'Sacred Passion', the suffering of Jesus made sacred by our inability to see it as our own, inflicted and inflicting, out of which a God who is all and only love, has brought our salvation, which reveals itself as a forgiveness for being 'human, all too human' (to quote Nietzsche), revealed as a strategy of human self-sufficiency, what Ernest Becker the agnostic wistfully called absolution by the absolute.

We have to learn our Christian belief again, as God's word to us in the forgotten and avoided language of ourselves and what we are really and shamefully about. We have to desacralise the Passion to reveal its victim anew in a real Gethsemani. We have to hear God speaking to us in the shameful way we keep order among ourselves.

Some revision! Especially in an age of terrorism when we are driven to think of violence as something we cannot do without. A cleansing revision! The Sacred Passion, desacralised to make it truly revelatory as the horror seen with Easter eyes, picks up on our sacred cows, of which the taboo on homosexuality is a glaring example, the unfamiliar out-lawed in the name of a violent order.

We get a line on this revision in the ambivalent attitude to it on the part of Urs von Balthasar. On the one hand he has said, 'who would have thought it would fall to an anthropologist to teach us theologians our business?' On the other hand, he faults Girard as seeing God as disap-proving of what was done to Jesus, against the tradition of the church which sees God accepting this enormity as an appeasing sacrifice. He upholds the Sacred Passion against the love that calls murder by its name in an act of incomprehensible forgiveness.

Eschaton

Jesus you let me see, and to my horror
The future of our human family:
Your church exultant, turned now to tomorrow
Will shudder in a new Gethsemani.

The way we live savours of our extinction,
We crucify ourselves – but here I pause:
You are the victim, there is no distinction:
Up on a cross we nail our primal cause.

And so the truth comes, and I catch my breath:
If how we live has put you on a cross
And you are you, risen to end our death,
What of our future and its certain loss?

This somehow you are giving me to see:
Your passion makes our end our ecstasy.

6.3 The Power and the Glory

New life in the risen body is lived without fear of death or imperial power, strengthened in silence.

With what were our first martyrs empowered and fearless? For answer, we must go to John's Gospel, in which Jesus gives us his mission statement. 'Other would-be shepherds have come only to grab and destroy. I have come for people to have life, and have it more abundantly.' Who are these other would-be leaders? In our age, we have had our fill of them, and the hideous ruin they have made, all serving their own *folie de grandeur* and leaving us with Auschwitz. And we cannot stop reading of the Nazi nightmare. They have appealed to the worst in people, the vengeful, escape from the ignominy of defeat. What Jesus offers is in the sharpest possible contrast to this leader's appeal: he calls it life more abundant.

Have we ever really asked what that could mean, in terms of life as we know it? What is this being-alive beyond our imagining? A step into this fuller life is being shown us in our time. Focusing lets the body speak and seek to befriend each other, not dominate, as our culture urges. Friendship is key. Friendship with Jesus, not now as the Galilean prophet but as he now is, the victim of world-violence risen from the dead to be the Everlasting Man in God. With *him* we are to be friends. In *him* we are to make friends. In him the martyrs are friends, their secret, life beyond death, life with no death in it, as God is.

Some scholars specialising in the early Christian writings are now finding between their words a consciousness explosion. And why wouldn't there be? How could there not be? *This* is the more abundant life he promised and left us wondering what it might be. He *promised* life unimaginably more, and here he was *delivering* what he promised, friendship with man in the bosom of God, man the Everlasting.

And we have access to him, we of the awakening west whom the Spirit, thoroughly secular now, is bringing through annihilation into limitless life, in the martyrial power of now. And we have a cloud of witnesses. The whole Catholic and wider mystical tradition is opening the heart to the more abundant life that Jesus risen called people into, so that their heart burned within them. It was not customary then to describe one's psychological state, but they did: they said, there he was, and our heart burned. It will burn today as it did then, if we will enter a blissful inner silence free of the deafening mental noise we are in, and learn slowly to be held in the power of now.

The more horrible the world becomes, the more we need the silence in us that is not escape but the intensification of spiritual energy. The silence is growing in us. It has only to connect with him.

How is it deathless, life that he has promised?
Well, where did death get in with other shepherds:
It was through rivalry, and he had none
But went for crucifixion and its issue
Which was eternal life, the world in God .
And silence beyond all imagination.

We are to live as if death were not
For it is now befriended in our silence
Freed of its link with rivalry and fear.
Death captured the apex of consciousness
Focus of all our insecurity
Exorcised in the night that Tolle knew
In terror, consciousness without its landmarks
To be surrendered to, nothing resisted
Of the dread void, peace beyond understanding.

6.4 No Fear

The whole church needs to overcome its fear of losing power, to listen and to speak confidently, addressing the anguish of division in the risen Body of Christ.

I have believed, therefore I have spoken[3]
There is, in the church today I believe, a state of fear. A state of fear in a specified body of people, such as the nation or the church or this or that community, is a difficult thing to write about. If I speak, for instance, of a state of fear in the church, many, indeed perhaps most, Catholics will ask me what I am talking about. But some, and perhaps many, will feel that they know. So it's a very slippery topic. Let me make a cast.

About ten years ago, Donald Cozzens, an American priest who had been for some time rector of a seminary, published a book called *Faith that Dares to Speak*,[4] in which he said that there was, abroad in the church, a fear of speaking out, and he was not referring to specific abuses such as the corruption of children, because it was 'faith' that he found afraid to speak, not things that have become issues, because people *are* talking about them. No, he was referring to the most radical thing in us, our faith, and it was of this that he thought people were afraid to speak. Say 'of church matters', and we come a bit closer. But which church matters?

Now Cozzens has a foreword to the very recent book by Bishop Geoffrey Robinson, the retired Australian canonist for the Diocese of Sydney. The book is called *Confronting Power and Sex in the Catholic Church: Reclaiming the Spirit of Jesus.*[5] So now we're getting more specific. The point is being made, by two eminent ecclesiastics together, that there exists a widespread fear to speak out on 'church matters', on matters where what we believe as Catholic Christians intersects with our lives as feeling sexual beings.

Now there is an interesting difference between Cozzens' book and his foreword to Robinson's recent book. Cozzens' book was, though passionately, annoyingly reluctant to specify. Doubtless he wanted what he had to say not to lose itself in 'issues', and this is important, because when one does become specific on church matters, the media are there with their hunger for news and their need for a living as journalists. So staying non-specific, in this slippery matter of fear, serves faith itself in its concrete reality undistracted by 'issues'. What the man is pointing to is the bare fact that a person's deeply personal Catholic faith finds itself tongue-tied among Catholics. There is a real faith that does not dare to speak, even to fellow-believers.

This is liable to be felt in religious (in the broadest sense) communities, among people, that is, who are 'professionally', as well as professed, Catholics. I certainly feel it in my own community, which has a long tradition of being comfortable with being Catholic. Many converts have found themselves at home here.

Now the *reason* why the unwillingness to speak out of faith is being felt in religious communities is that these are tied to the authority structure of the church in a way that your average Catholic is not. So we have to pursue our enquiry in the direction of this authority structure. How might fear come to be in the way authority feels itself vis-à-vis the church that it governs? Let me pursue a suggestion as to the answer.

What shape might fear take in those who hold power? Clearly it will be the fear of *losing* power, of not being in control of the church. This is rather outlandish language, because no one believes that 'the men in Rome' 'control' the church. But I am referring not to control as a status, but as something desired, wished-for, by those in authority. St Benedict is specific about the danger of an abbot's becoming nervous about the order in the house, 'for then he will never be at peace'.

So just suppose that the people in the Roman Curia who are the most liable to the unease that Benedict is talking about, that is, those most directly involved in the running of the church, suppose that these people feel their power threatened by the growing appeal to Vatican II as a promise felt to be unfulfilled. Certainly there is this pressure on Rome, and it is felt *in* Rome. Those who are exerting it have been referred to by an eminent scholar as 'aging sixties radicals', but they are exerting pressure, and pressure presumably is felt.

Now I'm going to try out a hypothesis. Just suppose that those in authority in the church today are feeling a loss of grip on the church as they see it. Theirs will be a state of fear, of a most radical kind, touching the very thing in which we all passionately believe. Now *this* fear will be communicating itself to people in the church, especially 'priests and nuns etc.'.

This passing-on of fear from the rulers to the ruled is surely a very ugly thing indeed. And if Roosevelt was right when he said that we have nothing to fear but fear itself, this has to be named and addressed. If we are picking up a fear felt by authority in the church, we are all in need of a big douche of Holy Spirit.

Let me take this a step further. If authority in the church is undergoing this inevitably communicated fear, this tells us something about the sort of faith that feels itself threatened with the loss of power. It is going to be not faith itself, not the vibrant living reality that faith is, but something thought of in propositions whose keeping in place is thought of as the essential mission of authority. And it is not for nothing that the now over-used term 'fundamentalism' comes from an American Protestant movement that would list propositions to be regarded as fundamental. There is a spiritual – certainly a spirited! – and emotional investment in formulas as the test of faith, which will characterise those in authority who feel their power threatened.

Now obviously we need to situate the fear of which I am speaking in the context of our present, post-conciliar church.

The Second Vatican Council has led to a radically new and different situation in our community, and, I suspect, in religious communities frequently, in which there came to be, in people's minds, two churches, one that you were in if you just went on thinking as you did in the beginning, another that people began to think in after the Council. Call this the church unchanged and the church changed and changing; the capital point is that it was a new church, a new claim on our adherence.

Now this was exactly what you expect to result from what happened. For what happened was that the new way of being church that clearly is implied in the great documents of the Council, and certainly the climate that came to be among the assembled bishops with their majorities amounting to virtual unanimity, was alive and well as long as the bishops were in Rome, but when they got home – certainly in this country, which is what we're talking about – they did not *explain* to us the sea change they had been through, they did not communicate it, expound it; in short, they did not take the steps that were necessary to show that the church, radically renewed, was still the one church there had always been. It took theologians to do this, and the bishops – certainly our Cardinal Heenan – were not theologians, and they did not employ theologians, as they had needed them at the Council, to explain the church renewed to people in this country. Just to labour the point, the bishops did not communicate 'the church renewed' to the people who would thus have been helped to see that it was still the church we were brought up in.

As nothing was done to acclimatize people to the renewed church, and people inevitably split into those enthusiastic for the new and those not at all enthusiastic, the notion of renewal has to be shown to be different from turning-into-something-else. Since this was not done, there resulted in people's minds two churches, the old and the new. There were two ways of being church mentally, and this is what we have had here ever since the Council. This cannot be sufficiently emphasised as unhealthy. It corrodes our faith.

From this unhappy state, there follows insecurity and fear, one member seeing another as in another church, or, more probably, wondering which church the other belongs to. And the only way to live with this situation is to keep quiet about it. This is a desperately unhealthy state for a community to be in, although, like everything that happens, people get used to it, and that is worse still, and corrosive of faith. Humans can normalise anything, as Germans got used to being Nazi and vaguely knowing about the camps.

We have come, no longer consciously, to live with these two inner churches and the implied injunction to keep it quiet, not to 'raise certain topics'. One day, in a homily at Mass, I said that I thought each of us has two Catholic Churches in mind, the pre-conciliar and the post-conciliar, and one of the community came up to me afterwards and thanked me for pointing this out. He said he had a lot of the old in him. This person is not by temperament at all crisis-minded, a practically rather than a theoretically oriented man.

Now obviously no one has both churches with the same intensity. That would be schizophrenic. He has his preferred church, with the other a worry, making for unhappiness with the church he thinks he is in. And above all, and never to be forgotten, the result of this lies in *the way we look at each other*, the way we look *to* each other. An old member of our community, long since dead, once said to me, in the course of a long drive – a well-known and well-tried way of communicating more honestly – that he always thought of Vatican II as a bad dream he hoped to wake up from. And all this comes of not being re-educated by the returning bishops in the new way of being the old church: in the world, not as a fortress with the world mistrusted.

And now there is an important further consideration. I have described what has happened here. We now must consider what has happened in Rome, in the papal curia. Now since the main thrust of the conciliar renewal was to require the reduction of the role of the curia from that of ruling court to that of implementing the government of the church by the bishops with the pope, there was going to be a strong resistance to this severe reduction of their role. The word conspiracy here is misleading. There is required only the habit of power to maintain itself, to stay in power. Only a clear-headed reforming pope could hope to change this. But far from doing this, the last Pope, over one of the longest reigns in church history, left the curia to carry on as usual while he lived as a pilgrim pope spreading the word in the world. The result was, as Nicholas Lash observes, that the church became more centralised in Rome than ever before in its history, with modern instant communication facilitating this, an ironic sequel to a Council that had tried to decentralise the church.

Now the mentality of the thus reinstated curia, the way in which its members continue to think, will not be to *discount* the Council, but to say that the Council itself changed nothing of importance. It merely reaffirmed what had always been, and this became a whole way of thinking. Even the present Pope, who is, exceptionally for the office, a world-class theologian, can say that the true interpretation of the Council is to see it as reaffirming, deepening, confirming, the church the way it has always been, and to see *as innovators* those theologians who insist that with the Council the church underwent a sea change from the fortress church to the church in the world.

So we have to see the community situation that I started with com-
pounded, powerfully and articulately, by this new Roman reduction of
the Council to a position no longer challenging or disturbing.

I suggest that when you add this factor to the already unhappy state
of the community mind that I set out to describe, the result is going to be
very serious indeed, and conducive to a state of fear corrosive of faith.
And the worst thing imaginable is a fear that one has got used to! *Libera
nos Domine!*

I do not pray in a divided church. I do not pray in one of two churches.
Nor do I think can anyone else. It has just occurred to me to wonder
whether this situation might somehow be addressed together, taking a
hint from what our latest retreat master has called 'an appreciative
examination'.

Now there is a *link* between fear in the church and authority in the
church. My supposition that for the curia, or 'the Vatican' – and there is a
problem with appropriate and non-emotive naming – 'fears losing
control' appears to be no more than a supposition – and rather cheeky –
until we look at what the Pope has to say about the Council.

Recently, in a crucial passage, the Pope characterised the different
interpretations of Vatican II in the following way:

> Problems in the implementation of the Council arose from the
> fact that two contrary hermeneutics came face to face and
> quarrelled with each other. One caused confusion, the other,
> silently but more and more visibly, bore and is bearing fruit.
> On the one hand, there is an interpretation that I would call 'a
> hermeneutic of discontinuity and rupture' ... On the other,
> there is the 'hermeneutic of reform', of renewal in the continu-
> ity of the one subject-Church which the Lord has given to us.
> She is a subject which increases in time and develops, yet
> always remaining the same, the one subject of the journeying
> People of God. The hermeneutic of discontinuity risks ending
> in a split between the pre-conciliar Church and the post-
> conciliar Church. It asserts that the texts of the Council as
> such do not yet express the true spirit of the Council. It claims
> that they are the result of compromises in which, to reach
> unanimity, it was found necessary to keep and reconfirm
> many old things that are now pointless. However, the true
> spirit of the council – they continue – is not to be found in

these compromises but instead in the impulses toward the new that are contained in the texts. These innovations alone were supposed to represent the true spirit of the council, and starting from and in conformity with them, it would be possible to move ahead. Precisely because the texts would only imperfectly reflect the true spirit of the council and its newness, it would be necessary to go courageously beyond the texts and make room for the newness in which the Council's deepest intention would be expressed, even if it were still vague. In a word: it would be necessary not to follow the texts of the Council but its spirit.[6]

In his new book, *Theology for Pilgrims*,[7] Nicholas Lash points accurately to what is disquieting in the Pope's account of the two ways of interpreting Vatican II. It is, that it is from the outset, in the description of the difference, polemical. Normally, when I say that there are two ways of approaching a profoundly significant document, you will assume that I am indicating two slants, two perspectives, each having something to be said for it. If I *start* by saying, 'there are two accounts of this matter, the bad one and the good won', we cease to be in a conversation and come under the myth of dominance, of 'I'm here to tell you!' Once the board is arranged this way, we are not surprised to find that, by 'new, innovative', our interpreter means 'disruptive'.

Lash then goes on, logically, to ask: who are these disruptive, novelty-pursuing people? These enemies are not participants in the conversation about Vatican II. They are people bent on pulling the documents their way, the way of disruptive novelty. And the casualty here is the word 'new', deprived of its implication of renewal and tradition-based growth, and firmly associated with 'novelty'. I keep recalling the fine phrase of Ezra Pound, 'Make it new!'

It is with this introduction of the controlling myth of dominance, the enemy of conversation, that the new comes to imply the inventive, the disruptive and, from the point of view of authority, the disturbing.

And of course, when it is the Pope who is addressing the crucial problem of interpretation in the controversial matter of the Council, we listen keenly, hoping to hear in his words the voice of friendly conversation indicating the desire to work with others for the reform of the papacy; we are especially sensitive to the intrusive myth of dominance – to put it crudely, 'to listen for some indication of coming off the high horse'. We are sad to hear, from the Pope, 'the same old thing', even in a more sophisticated language. To put it crudely, we are to gather that the Pope is on the side of the curia, whose unremitting resistance to reform is a constant theme in the minutes of the Council, and – to lapse again into polemic – raises the whole question of the history of the Council. The history is in the minutes. The minutes afford a dynamic, not a static history of the Council that features them as indicators of resistance to the movement of the Council. The minutes are not something to be *refuted*, as Bishop Marchetti is doing in his new book recently launched in Rome, with curial if not papal support. You don't refute the minutes of a meeting: you may *dispute* them if you think they are inaccurate. Bishop Marchetti's book is a sustained attack on the *History of Vatican II*, edited by Giuseppe Alberigo, compared by John O'Malley SJ with Jedin's *History of the Council of Trent*. If it is a story of resistance to reform kept up by those who represent the status quo, this is to be expected. It is of the nature of long-settled power.

Surely there is this link between the state of affairs that I find in religious communities today and the state of things in Rome. The feeling, perhaps mistaken, that the Pope is against reform, is resisting the new, sends fear through the whole body which wants to be alive in the love of Christ as it confidently addresses the anguish of this time.

No fear

What could be worse than an unnoticed fear
The slow poison of a community
Whose origin seems far as well as near
Accepting new directives tacitly.

God save us from monastic taciturn
By reawaking love in us from where
You rise for ever for the heart to burn
With love that we profess to cast out fear.

How we are one in Christ is charity
And not by rulings given from above,
Honesty must be between you and me
And caring from the heart's initial move.

No clever couplet, your reality
Comforts with nothing making the heart free.

6.5 Love your Enemies and Enjoy it

New life without fear, lived in the consciousness of the resurrection, means more than just hearing each other speak. It means becoming a loving outsider, like the Good Samaritan, like Christ himself. It means identifying with the enemy and befriending the victim.

The Great Parable

Today we celebrate St Bonaventure, who gave to medieval scholasticism a strong turn from an intellectual to a love-centred understanding. I want to commemorate him personally by an understanding given me by a recent homily of Fr Leo's, into the greatest of all the parables, the Good Samaritan, the Loving Outsider.

Who was neighbour to the man who was beaten up and left for dead? And who is asking that question? The man the world beat up and left dead, whom God has raised to life free of death's dominion. So what the parable is saying is: be a Samaritan, be an outsider to this world of dominance and death, join the victim, and you will be alive in a new world that God brings to life in his Son, crucified in this world and alive in God's world that is not shaped by death as ours is. We need this vision now, when the church is bewildered by scandals and needs to hear the words of Paul, 'if you are raised up with Christ, think above this world and do not be terrorised by it. There is no condemnation for those who are in Christ Jesus, who are neighbour to the world's victim dead and risen for ever.'[8] I have to ask: am I neighbour to the victim, to him who 'looked for help and there was no one'? The parable states the inversion of a too familiar world. It invites us into a new consciousness.

At school, did I ever side with someone who was being badly bullied? Never, but I knew one or two who did. You could call them the moral aristocrats, us the moral pygmies. To identify with someone who is being victimized is to be on the way of the risen victim, which is the way to eternal life. To side with the victim, who is the risen one, is to be on the road to heaven. This is the parable of the loving outsider who finds himself on that road. It is the heart of the parables. Take it to heart!

Love your enemies and enjoy it

Our desperate need today is for a new consciousness, a new awareness. Not a sharper or a clearer or a better awareness, or an awareness of more, but a new awareness. In all our experience, there is the experi-

encer, the you you never notice, open to God in the silence that the new
atheists are filling with the mental noise of their angry words. Feel your
silence, and you might even find yourself praying for them, poor men.

When Jesus says 'love your enemies and pray for those who persecute
you!' and you take this straight, it involves a huge effort of will, a
decision through clenched teeth. But for the new awareness this is an
invitation to relax, it means resilience, moving in harmony with the sun
that rises on all, not fussy as in *Under Milk Wood*: 'and if you let the sun
in, see that he wipes his boots!'

There are a few people we know about who have stumbled, tumbled,
into this new self-awareness. But it waits on you, in an ordinary way.
Take the words 'be still, and know that I am God!' and say them to
yourself slowly, pausing at the comma. For the first time, notice in your
experience the experiencer, you. The purpose of having a stretch of
prayer-time or *lectio*, is to give the new consciousness a chance to
become stronger, more available to you at any time. In prayer, you give
the new awareness a chance to become a tenderness, and this is likely to
be there when something annoying happens.

One of the fruits of the new awareness is that you can look at
outlandish behaviour on the part of public figures without that awful
indignation that stops all real thinking. When the top cardinal in the
Vatican liturgy department, in an interview in London, replies that there
shall be a Tridentine Mass, 'not in some parishes but in all parishes',
don't explode! Treat it as burlesque. There is a way of relaxation open to
you that has its roots in the eternity that loves you into being. So go with
the flow, and let the cardinal go too.

> No more food now for my disgruntlement,
> Identify with him who takes it all
> Up into the eternal firmament
> If I will only hear the victim call,
>
> Be the outsider and the victim's neighbour
> Who is to lift us all where death is not,
> Whose certain lightening of all our labour
> Is the sign of all those of God begot.
>
> Now be a Presence in a foul milieu
> That death conveys to fear its concubine:
> There is the other way we may prefer
> Of which the risen Victim is the sign.

Befriend the Victim who has won the day
Is how to live and living so to pray.

6.6 Eternal Banquet

The way we live has had God for its victim, and so it has God for our saviour from it. The new creation transformed in Christ overcomes our exploitation of each other and of the planet, renewing heaven and earth. God keeps on helping us to get there.

At a dinner party to which Jesus was invited, a member of the order of Pharisees indulges in a piece of gastronomic eschatology and murmurs: how pleasant it will be to dine in the Kingdom to come. And Jesus says, 'Don't be so sure! There'll be surprises.'

Today the church, at a rather sleepy liturgy, looks forward to a sort of transfigured permanent Eucharist. But this time, the warning, 'don't be so sure!' comes from science as it predicts an early extinction of the human race as a species incapable of inhabiting a planet which, instead of inhabiting peacefully, it has abused.

Somehow our faith requires that we put one on top of the other these two images, of our self-destruction and a new heaven and a new earth.

This putting-together is inescapable. No longer does our theology, awake to the resurrection of Jesus as our human future beginning, allow us the old penny catechism sidestep into eternity with our immortal soul, crowned with a private heaven.

Now here is a way that comes to me for putting the two images together.

By the way we run the world, the way of violence, scapegoating and victimage, we are cooperating with our extinction as a species – recall Shakespeare's prophetic vision in *King Lear*, that 'humanity must perforce prey on itself/Like monsters of the deep'.[9] But now we are being shown a new consciousness that is the reverse of this self-destructive way of running the world. Only by tuning in to the crucified and risen one are we to know that this new consciousness is of God our creator and redeemer. In brief, the way we live has had God for its victim, and so it has God for our saviour from it.

But it is faith alone that holds the two images together, the scientific one of extinction, the Christian one of a new heaven and a new earth.

Only faith, contemplatively fixed upon Jesus, put to death by our violent way of being in the world, and raised to life as a divine swallowing-up of our violence in love.

More briefly, you have to love people enough in faith and hope to want heaven as an eternal banquet. Loving people means waking from a mindless existence that is grounded in violence. It means the transition from 'the myth of dominance' to the light that is Christ.

And then suddenly it bursts upon me. In the attempt to reconcile the scientific vision of a planet abused by our violent self-indulgence, and the heart-enflaming sight of the risen one, I am perforce identifying our abuse of our planetary home with Jesus violated on the cross. That butchered and bloody figure epitomises our abuse of the earth. As Richard Rohr OFM says, contemplating the crucifix, 'See what we do to beauty!' See what we are doing to the earth!

In this vision, of the crucified planet, there come together the two vectors, of science and faith. What we might call the 'church churlish', the church with her back toward the Enlightenment and the Declaration of the Rights of Man, is finally to turn round.

At such a turning, how does sex look? Or rather, how does the church's traditional picture of sex look? Very briefly, like a necessary evil, necessary for the propagation of the race. Sex as the sacrament of love that unites where so much of our living tears in pieces has yet to find a place in doctrine. It is grudgingly accepted for partners sworn together for life without access to contraception, rejected everywhere else that creation has placed it.

But a true vision of sexuality in Christ will be as exacting as a true vision of our planetary home in Christ. To say that 'anything goes!' for sex would be enunciating a policy for sex that has been our implicit policy for planetary exploitation: anything goes!

The church's traditionally selective interest in sex has reflected a selective interest in the planet, useful for our convenience, not our given partner in a relationship we are born into. Our life 'on earth' has been as selective *of earth* as our dabbling in our erotic energies.

Calvary and its triumphal sequel has been, hitherto, the human drama *on the human stage*. In the vision that science now unfolds, there *is* no stage, only the fate of the human species through neglect of its habitat. But once the murder of Christ has been seen as the sum of our mutual violence that is *co-operative with our extinction*, we see the victim's response as our transformation into love. So that in the crucifixion/ resurrection, freshly revealed in the Spirit to our scientifically troubled age, we see a Christ who is, as he ever was, cosmic, and not only human in his significance.

I come back to my suggested formula. If the way we live, exploitatively, has the Son of God for its victim, it has him, creative Logos, for its transformer.

Three unlikely allies emerge from these ruminations: Whitman, Hopkins and Lawrence. Whitman's 'thou dark rondure swimming in space'; Hopkins' 'dearest freshness deep down things … Holy Spirit over the bent World broods … with (Ah) bright wings'; Lawrence's *Sons and Lovers*.

The Good Seed and the Bad

The genius of many of the parables is that they cannot be understood or applied without wisdom. Milton used the parable of the seed to write the *Areopagitika*, a polemic for free speech, a document I wouldn't know about if I had not had to take a reluctant fifth form through it for the public exams.

Only wisdom can know if and when to interfere, and for this gift of the Holy Spirit we are abjectly dependent on the Holy Spirit and prayer. Our last government affords a good example of inattention to this parable, piling legislation on legislation and encouraging children not to take risks.

How beautiful is God's hidden action in the world, creating continually out of nothing and surprising. Charles Taylor, the most profound Catholic thinker today, compares God to a superb tennis-player who can always return the serve, however skewed. The Samaritan's action is part of God's response to the skewed serve that the robbers have lobbed into history.

Now to go with God is what we call wisdom, and for this Taylor says that the Gospel affords a better anthropology than the Greeks who gave us soul and body. For this anthropology, the essential is the heart, which is either of flesh or of stone. I mentioned this the other day to an old friend and she said, 'I have a heart of stone and I'm always asking God to replace it with flesh.' Hear hear!

So this is how to work with God, attention to today's parable about interference. I think that if we let God do in us what the prophet Ezekiel is talking about, we'd do so much better and do less harm in the world, to say nothing of beginning to understand the generosity that makes that which is not to be that which is. We screw up, and he creates anew. Blessed be God!

6.7 The Gospel Deprofessionalised

The new creation has already begun. Good news for everyone – the 'gospel deprofessionalised' – is the simple fact that we are loved out of nothing into being. How can our hearts hear this? By following the Spirit into a future yet unknown.

Cor ad cor loquitur

'Ratzinger's deeply Trinitarian anthropology emphasises the importance of relationality – that dimension of the person which makes him or her unique and unrepeatable. He has written that the era of defining the person solely in terms of substantiality (those elements human persons share) is over.'[10] This involves a rediscovery of the person as loved out of nothing into being.

Now the Pope stands for a theological basis that is 'of the heart'. His long-time love for the mind of Newman – *cor ad cor loquitur* – shows this.

The question is, though, how, in the world as it is today with its currents of violence and ecclesiastically deplored 'secularism', *does* the heart speak to the heart? This of course is putting the question far too vaguely. The question is more like: how might the heart, animated by a profound sense of being loved into being, speak to the heart?

The point is, I think, that all the words of approval for a heart-centred understanding of the human condition take place in the hothouse of theology. And a review of Ratzinger's book, *Jesus of Nazareth*, finds that he does not go on to follow the Spirit right out into the world and life and the things that the world gets into, the quagmires and the brilliant discoveries. He stays with the Spirit in the church. One of the most refreshing things about the book – and this is unique today – is that he offered it as his personal opinion as a theologian, not as Pope.

The *voice* of the Loving One in such a world as ours is a voice in our language. The work that has to be done in and by the church is to help this voice of one surprised into being to hear itself in the accents of the crucified and risen victim of our violence. For it has been pointed out that the world already recognises a Jesus who represents suffering humanity in God. If the heart speaks to the heart the one language of love, suffering is a universal language that recognises a divine victim.

In a review, in the *Times Literary Supplement*, of Pope Benedict's book, *Jesus of Nazareth*, Fr Peter Cornwell made an interesting point. He said that the author sees the Holy Spirit as *confirmatory* of what has been, of all that the church has been down the ages. There is, he pointed out, another understanding of the Spirit, as urging toward the future that is unknown, and this is surely the direction of the Spirit in our time. As quoted, the Pope sees Vatican II as subject to two interpretations, a hermeneutic of confirmation and a hermeneutic of disruption. But where does the Holy Spirit show up as between these two? Surely the Third Person shows a third way, a new consciousness freshly alive to the cosmic reality we are in, *as* its awareness. We need to get out of the theological hothouse.

A few years ago, James Alison, one of the most creative theologians of our time, said to me, 'You know, only once in our day has the voice of Christian theology broken in on the culture: when John Robinson the Bishop of Woolwich wrote *Honest to God*. Then *the world* heard that for God we must look not without or above but within.'

Never was this deprofessionalising of the Gospel more needed than in the church just now, when the scandal of child abuse is inducing a horrible atmosphere of fear and suspicion that is corrosive. We need an Isaiah to say to us: stiffen weakened knees!

The call

The time I took my life into my prayer
Was when I said to you, simply, you bore me
For then it happened, you were everywhere
And my life suddenly no longer stormy.

The self within and what I call my life
Became identical and I was new
The preferential option for the strife
Dissolved as you gave me yourself as you.

This is the bliss that waits upon us all
Who have to learn a self no longer two,
The dualism that prevents the call
From coming through to the deep self from you

To tell us as no one on earth is able
That we are loved, and not otherwise stable.

Notes

1: Thursday Evening: Broken Bread, Broken Bodies

1. J. Kirkpatrick, *In Breaking of Bread: The Eucharist and Ritual* (Cambridge University Press, 1993).
2. 'O sacred banquet', the splendid composition of Aquinas.
3. Louis-Marie Chauvet, *Symbol and Sacrament: a Sacramental Reinterpretation of Christian Existence* (Collegeville, MN: Liturgical Press, 1995), p. 315.
4. See Chapter 3 on Girard and sacrifice.
5. Max Scheler (1874–1928), *On the Eternal in Man*, trans. Bernard Noble (London: SCM Press, 1960).
6. Eamon Duffy, 'Benedict XVI and the Eucharist', *New Blackfriars* (March 2007), p. 202.
7. As quoted in Duffy, 'Benedict XVI and the Eucharist'.
8. London: Dacre Press, 1945.
9. *Summa Theologiae* 3.73.5, quoted here by P. F. Fitzpatrick in *In Breaking of Bread*.
10. Northrop Frye, *Fearful Symmetry: A Study of William Blake* (1947; new edition, University of Toronto Press, 2004).
11. For example, in *Our Final Century: Will the Human Race Survive the Twenty-first Century?* (London: William Heinemann, 2003).
12. *Confessions* VII.16.
13. *Republic* 361e 5.
14. J.-M. Oughourlian, *The Puppet of Desire: The Psychology of Hysteria, Possession, and Hypnosis*, trans. Eugene Webb (Palo Alto, CA: Stanford University Press, 1991).

2: Thursday Night – The Void in the Garden

1. For an introduction to Eckhart Tolle's thought see *The Power of Now: A Guide to Spiritual Enlightenment* (London: Hodder, 2001), or *A New Earth: Awakening to Your Life's Purpose* (London: Penguin, 2006).
2. See John Chapman, *Spiritual Letters* (1935; London: Continuum, 2003).

3. Luke 22:42–44 (italics added) from *Good As New: A Radical Retelling of the Scriptures* (Ropley: O Books, 2004).
4. See *A New Earth*, pp. 100ff.
5. From *Andrea del Sarto* (1855).
6. *Confessions* I.1.
7. *Jesus of Nazareth* (ET London: Bloomsbury, 2007).
8. René Le Senne (1882–1934), *Obstacle et Valeur: La description de conscience* (Paris: Aubier, 1934).
9. Presentation for the 2009 Theology and Peace Conference, held at St Mary's University College, Twickenham. See www.jamesalison.co.uk/texts/eng57/html.

3: Friday Afternoon – Broken Body on the Cross

1. See René Girard, *Violence and the Sacred*, new edition (London: Continuum, 2005).
2. John Clifford Henson, *Good As New: A Radical Reading of the Scriptures* (Ropley: O Books, 2004).
3. J. B. Metz, *Faith in History and Society: Toward a Fundamental Practical Theology* (London: Burns and Oates, 1980), e.g. p. 171.
4. J. D. Zizioulas, *Communion and Otherness: Further Studies in Personhood and Church* (London: T&T Clark, 2007).
5. The two disciples on the road to Emmaus.
6. *Mensonge romantique et vérité Romanesque* (1961), ET *Deceit, Desire and the Novel: Self and Other in Literary Structure* (Baltimore, MD: Johns Hopkins Press, 1965).
7. *Deceit, Desire and the Novel*, p. 59.
8. See '*O Sacrum Convivium*' in Chapter 1.2.
9. By Lionel Shriver, Berkeley, CA: Counterpoint Press, 2003.
10. Max Scheler, *On the Eternal in Man*, trans. B. Noble (New York: Harper, 1960).
11. Subtitled *Women, Sexuality, and the Catholic Church*, trans. Peter Hennessy (Harmondsworth: Penguin, 1991).
12. *Kleriker: Psychogramm eines ideals* (1989).

4: Saturday Night – The Tomb in the Garden

1. Martin Hengel, *The Son of God: The Origin of Christianity and the History of Jewish-Hellenistic Religion* (1975, ET, trans. J. Bowden, London: SCM Press, 1976); Larry W. Hurtado, 'Early Devotion to Jesus', *Expository Times* 122/4 (2010), pp. 167–76
2. Quoted from A. O. Dyson, *Who Is Jesus Christ?* (London: SCM Press, 1969), p. 78 – a book long out of print I am sure.

5: Sunday Morning – Transformed Body

1. George Lakoff, *The Political Mind: Why You Can't Understand 21st-Century American Politics with an 18th-Century Brain* (New York: Viking, 2008); as paperback, *The Political Mind: A Cognitive Scientist's Guide to Your Brain and Its Politics* (London: Penguin, 2009).

2. N. T. Wright, *The Resurrection of the Son of God* (London: SPCK, 2003).
3. *The Resurrection Effect: Transforming Christian Life and Thought* (Maryknoll, NY: Orbis Books, 2008).
4. Kelly, *The Resurrection Effect*.
5. Exciting new findings in neuroscience, by George Lakoff, University of Berkeley, California: 'A new Enlightenment must go deeper than the debate based on normal conscious understanding. What is normally unconscious must be made conscious. And political debate needs to be informed by the sciences of the brain and the mind, as these sciences develop.' See *The Political Mind* (note 1 above).
6. From 'Correspondances', in *Fleurs du Mal* (1857).

6: Next Week – Beyond the Garden

1. James Alison, *Broken Hearts and New Creations: Intimations of a Great Reversal* (London: Darton, Longman and Todd, and New York: Continuum, 2010).
2. Søren Kierkegaard said, memorably, that life is lived forward but understood backward. The rower has his back to where he is going. And then there's Woody Allen: 'If you want to make God laugh, tell him your plans!'
3. Psalm 116:10.
4. *Faith that Dares to Speak* (Collegeville, MN: Liturgical Press, 2004).
5. Dublin: The Columba Press, 2007.
6. Christmas Address of His Holiness Benedict XVI to the Roman Curia, 22 December 2005.
7. London: Darton, Longman and Todd, 2008.
8. See Colossians 3:1 and Romans 8:1.
9. Act 4, sc. 2.
10. Article by Tracy Rowland in *The Tablet* for 9 July 2010.

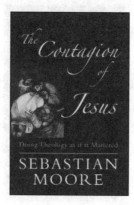

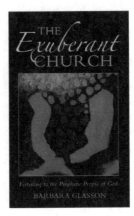